WHY GOD WHY

"Consider it all joy, my brethren, when you encounter various trials, knowing that the testing of your faith produces endurance. And let endurance have its perfect result, so that you may be perfect and complete, lacking in nothing."– **James 1:2-4**

WHY GOD WHY?

Did You Ever Wonder Why This is Happening to Me?

VIOLET HAMILTON

WHY GOD WHY?

© 2017 by Violet Hamilton

No part of this publication may be reproduced or transmitted in any form or by any means, mechanical or electronic, including photocopying and recording, or by any information storage and retrieval system, without permission in writing from the author or publisher (except by a reviewer, who may quote brief passages and/or brief video clips in a review).

The scanning, uploading and distribution of this book via the Internet or via any other means without the permission of the author or publisher is illegal and punishable by law. Please purchase only authorized electronic editions, and do not participate in or encourage electronic piracy of copyrighted materials.

ISBN: 978-1-937925-19-2 PAPERBACK

Published by:

Forest, VA
PublishersSolution.com
Cover & Interior Design by the Publishers Solution Team

Author photo *(Pg 175)* by Jack Henley
Portrait Design
www.jackhenley.com

DEDICATION

To my husband, Harvey, for stalking me until I noticed him. And for encouraging me, through our journey, to take the road less traveled.

To my daughter, Wendy, for sixteen wonderful years of love and joy. For always reminding us of the important things in life. Her commitment to the Lord Jesus and her love for others was a true testimony of who Wendy was.

To my son, Tim, for walking with us through the valley and mountain-top experiences. For bringing to our family, the cream-of-the-crop daughter-in-law, who together sacrificed their journey to come to our rescue.

To my daughter-in-law, Laura, who keeps the family marching to a positive drummer, and who insists—"Hamilton's never quit."

To my grandchildren, Wyatt, Sam and Nora, for adding life's joyful and sustaining ingredients.

To my long-time friend, Deda Bohannon, for encouraging and prompting me until I started writing the book.

To Michelle King, and the late, Niki Bohan, for the long hours of proofing.

To my God-sent friend, Gail Eatman, for pushing me to the end.

To Jack Henley for gifting our photography needs.

ACKNOWLEDGEMENT

Rise Again by Dallas Holm. All rights reserved. Lyrics reprinted by permission. 1977 Dove Awards: Song of the Year (Rise Again), Songwriter of the Year, Male Vocalist of the Year, Mixed Group of the Year (Dallas Holm and Praise).

Thank you for allowing me to share the lyrics that have been so inspirational to our family.

CONTENTS

Foreword xi
Introduction ix

Chapters

1 God, Please Don't Take My Children 1
2 Predestined Soul Mates 15
3 What Fairytale Life? 23
4 Transformation and Creation 31
5 The Abandoned Well 37
6 He Prayed, God Listened 41
7 Why Suicide 45
8 Have They Been Kidnapped? 51
9 The Sacrificial Gift 55
10 Mother Buried Her Unhealed Wounds 59
11 Why Five Years to the Day? 67
12 An Upside Day with a Downhill End 71
13 Unforgiving Trip to Denver 75

WHY GOD WHY?

14	From Holy Ground to Holy Terror	79
15	He Gave Us the Green Light, We Gave Him the Glory	85
16	Angels Playing in the Clouds	89
17	The Lost Bible	95
18	Our Special Blessing from Brazil	99
19	Near Death, and So Far from Home	103
20	His Timing, Not Mine	109
21	Double Whammy!	113
22	Elvis Is Dead	117
23	Beyond Mentoring	121
24	A Spontaneous Vacation with Adventure	127
25	Two Super Genes Unite	135
26	We're Going to Crash	139
27	From a Cruise to the Emergency Room	143
28	The Propeller Is Going!	149
29	The Grandfather	153
30	When You think, You Have Troubles…	163
31	Do It Again, Grandfather	167
32	Did You Ever Wonder Why?	171

About the Author 175

FOREWORD

Be prepared to laugh, to cry, to reflect, and to be inspired. Violet Hamilton touches us all in her book, *"Why God Why?"* She shares her journey, inviting the reader along for the ride. It's a love story, detailing how she met and married Harvey. Her book is about living, drinking in the essence of life; embracing it in its entirety. She paints a word picture about the survival of the human spirt; a woman, a wife, a mother, a business woman, and a Christian.

It has been my privilege to know the Hamilton family for nearly four decades. I first became acquainted with them when I served as a youth pastor of their daughter, Wendy. I was struck by her spiritual maturity and sensitivity to others. She was beyond her years in insight. You're not supposed to have "favorites" but Becky, my wife, and I could not help but feel a special connection to her.

I was speaking to several hundred high schoolers in the front gym of the Thomas Road Baptist Church when a note was passed to me. "Wendy Hamilton has been in an accident, pray," it stated. Soon afterward, her tragic and unexpected death impacted all of us. The Scripture states, *"That I might know him and the power of his resurrection and the fellowship of his suffering."* There is something powerful about sharing the "suffering" experience at the loss of someone so young. Amidst that suffering there is something supernatural about sharing the "power" of His resurrection in the aftermath of healing in the acceptance of such loss. Violet eloquently and intimately opens the window of her soul to share her loss and her healing of Wendy's home going.

WHY GOD WHY?

The Bible offers, *"Whatsoever was written aforetime was written for our learning that we through patience of the scriptures may have hope."* The Scriptures are a collection of divine stories given for the benefit of readers' encouragement. In this manner, Violet transparently invites us to experience her life of "special stories" that will touch all who read them.

Thank you, Violet, for putting to pen, *"Why God Why?"* My life has been enriched by your successful record of God's work in and through you. "You are an epistle known and read of all men." Your life is one that puts Christ on display amidst your journey. No doubt, this book will be used by our Lord to touch the lives of countless.

I am honored to have been a small part in that journey.

Dr. Dave Adams
Director of Pastoral Leadership
Professor of Pastoral Ministry
School of Divinity, Liberty University
Lynchburg, Virginia

INTRODUCTION

Honestly, this was not the book that I had convinced myself to write. Out of concern, I had decided to write about newlyweds and their acceptance as a new member by the family. There were many stories of them feeling like outsiders, and that didn't sit right with me.

My sweet husband, Harvey, drove me through the beautiful Blue Ridge Mountains. The views were breathtaking, including the yearly Rhododendron that was in full bloom. I laid my face against the window peering at the sun rays streaking through the clouds. My mind was passive until God began to fill it with a clear directive about writing my book. It was far from the subject I had thought about inking an hour ago. Curiously, I followed His voice, as it seemed to come from the clouds. Pictures of our marriage and past family events began to roll through my head. It also included our valley experiences, and how we survived the many tragedies that had befallen us. One simple sentence was very clear; "Others need to hear." No other directions followed. However, the message grew stronger and stronger over the next few days.... then the next few weeks, but I continued to make excuses.

Confiding in my good friend didn't help get me off the hook. "Violet, you and Harvey have been through so many life experiences, you really should obey and write your story. Others do need to know how you two survived, stayed mentally stable and are still together. Not only that, tell them of all the wonderful and funny things you have experienced." "How can I write about Wendy's death," I cried. She quickly reminded me that,

WHY GOD WHY?

when the Lord gives you a directive, He will give you the means to act…. He will give you the strength and the words as you write. Losing my sixteen-year-old child was the most devastating experience in my life. I wanted to tell others how the Lord walked with us through each and every day of our sorrow. He took my hand many times, and I could feel His scars deep in the palms. That brought me through the valley with restoration. Also, confident that Wendy knew and loved Jesus, and she is rejoicing in heaven consoled my spirit and mind.

It was during a vacation that Harvey and I settled in a cabin, high up in the mountains of Tennessee that God spoke to me once again. The views of the Smokey Mountains and gorgeous valleys below were awesome. It was so peaceful and quiet that Harvey could work on his music renditions. On the other hand, I was enjoying the hot tub on the deck, while listening to the waterfall. In my relaxed state, I leaned back against the headrest. A few minutes had passed, when my relaxed mind began to fill rapidly. Ideas for my book overflowed with past events of our journey. Immediately, I jumped out of the hot tub, wrapped myself in a towel and ran to my computer. My fingers were flying as I recorded these thoughts that seemed vivid as a picture. The Lord motivates with quick and direct nudges. For four hours, I typed non-stop with no format or spell check, just line-for-line entry. At times my heart sank as I recalled the unexpected tragedies in our family. I realized the book needed to include the good times, the funny times and the unusual times. I switched it up to include memorable events that made me laugh and cry at the same time.

Procrastinating so many years made it harder, but I am so thankful He continued to nudge me until I obeyed. One thing I learned: when the Lord tells you to act on something, it's best to obey. I sincerely pray that this book will help others to know what I have learned over a lifetime; to draw their strength and hope from God alone. Whether on the mountaintop or in the valley, we should rejoice and give God alone the glory.

Chapter 1
GOD, PLEASE DON'T TAKE MY CHILDREN!

Chilled by the sound of sirens on the highway, this dreary Sunday morning of October 5, 1980, changed our lives forever. As I began to dress for church, my thoughts were with those possibly involved in an accident. The children had been gone for some time now, so I didn't worry about them. Jackie, Wendy's friend, had spent the night and wanted Wendy to drive her home to get clothes for church. Wendy was only sixteen and had just obtained her driver's license; hence, Harvey reluctantly granted this request. We had driven with Wendy for months, and she had proven to be an excellent driver. Tim, our six-year-old, begged to go with the girls and jumped in the back seat before I could answer. He was so excited that I didn't make waves. "Please be careful," I yelled as they drove away.

A short while later, there was an unexpected knock on the kitchen door. A neighbor, with the most devastating expression on his face, asked Harvey to come outside. I became very nervous as I watched from the kitchen window. To my surprise, they quickly drove off in the neighbor's car without saying a word. While I stood in the driveway, in anticipated fear, Papa Hamilton drove up. His face was white, his head hung down, and he trembled as he explained, "Wendy and Tim have been in a bad accident on the highway." Papa happened to be traveling behind the other

WHY GOD WHY?

vehicle involved. Although he was in no condition to drive, I begged him to take me to see the children. Thankfully, my sister-in-law, Pat pulled in the driveway, and quickly drove me to the accident.

Approaching the scene, I could see two cars so terribly crushed that my heart began to race, and my throat felt like it was swelling. Frantically, I started looking for the children. Tim's teacher, Mrs. Ellis, had driven by just after the accident and helped Papa the best she could. He was so shaken that he asked her to wait with Tim until his dad arrived. By the time Pat and I got there, the rescue squad had taken the children to the hospital, along with Harvey and his mother. My worst nightmare was beginning to unfold, and my stomach was about to empty out. In agony, I cried and prayed all the way to the hospital, "God, please don't take my children!" I tried reasoning with Him one moment and begging the next. For an instant, I felt a sweet, spiritual fervor around me. Calming down a little, I lay my head against the window and prayed, "Lord, please give Harvey and me the faith and strength to face whatever is in store for us. Take my hand, Lord, and hold me up when I begin to fall."

Pat pulled up to the emergency door where Harvey and his friend, Wayne were standing. Harvey ran over and grabbed me before I entered the hospital. I felt him trying to protect me when he detained me to speak of the children's condition. However, his voice could not hide the seriousness on his face. "Honey, Tim is being sutured and treated for lacerations and stomach problems." His voice began to tremble; "Wendy is unconscious with a severe head injury. They are waiting for the neurologist's prognosis on her condition and chance of survival." "Survival? Survival?" I questioned! Jackie was treated for cuts to her back. Then both Tim and Jackie were being X-rayed for additional injuries. I became weak, and my stomach was in knots, as I clung to Harvey for support. Uncontrollable groaning came from my being as if my feelings and my expressions were not in sync.

When we saw Tim, we found that he was stitched from head to toe and was constantly throwing up from the trauma. The nursing staff asked us to leave while they attended to him. We desperately wanted to see Wendy but were told that attendants were working arduously on her. We would have to wait.

By the time Jackie's Mom and Dad arrived at the hospital, we were in a small holding room anxiously waiting to see our children. Harvey informed them of the children's condition; "Jackie and Tim are out of danger, but there is concern about Wendy," he tearfully communicated. An hour had passed without a word from the staff, and I just could not wait any longer. "Harvey, I have to see her and know that she is okay. Please do something!" The nurse finally agreed to let us see her briefly. It was worse than I thought. Wendy was unconscious, blood running from her nose, and her beautiful face was swollen. Completely devastated, Harvey and I could not console one another. We read each other's mind and confirmed that we had to release Wendy to God's care and let His will be done. Still, the fear I presented on my face exhibited fear in my heart.

The nurses finally moved us upstairs to a room closer to where they were observing Wendy. We didn't know they had moved her from the emergency room. Tim had already been admitted to the hospital. The medical team had a concern because of his head injury and prolonged nausea. I was overwhelmed. "Lord, please give me strength, otherwise, take me home with you. This pain in my heart and soul is more than I can endure."

My sweet friends, Jimmy and Mary Thomas, came to console us and help in any way they could. Their message to me was very clear, but yet, consoling. Mary sat down beside me, and with her whole heart said, "Violet, we don't know the outcome for Wendy, but she is in the hands of Jesus. Whether He decides to heal her brain or take her home, she will continue to be in His hands." Those words reassured me that He is our Father, the almighty, powerful, loving God. If His overall plan included

WHY GOD WHY?

taking Wendy to heaven, I knew I had to let her go, but I was not ready and needed more time.

Many church members, family, and friends began to come. They were directed to a waiting room. Mother had asked the doctor for something to help calm my nerves. A prescription was filled, and someone inserted pills into my mouth, followed by water. I was so numb by this time I hardly knew what they were doing. My mother had always been there for answers, but this time, she needed answers. Mama and Papa Hamilton and Pat were trying to be strong and very supportive. From witnessing the accident and seeing Wendy in such a state, Papa would have a fractured memory that would stay with him forever.

When my sisters, Jan and Sheilla, entered the room, I felt a secure shield of family, as if they were circling the wagons to keep me from danger. Although they were at a loss for words, their presence gave me a light of courage. We all prayed and waited for information on Wendy.

It was all I could do to hold back my tears when we went downstairs to check on Tim. Wayne offered moral support, as he followed Harvey for hours. Our long-time friends, Deda and Johnny, were at our home cleaning up the mess from breakfast and preparing for the worse. As always, they had been there in all of our times of need. Support from loving friends and family means so much in times like these.

It was quite warm in the room, and the medication was making me feel lifeless. My thoughts drifted back to our years with Wendy. She had grown to be the most beautiful young lady, inside and out. She loved people, especially children, and cared moreover about their relationship with the Lord. She notably gave attention to the underdogs (less popular kids). For some reason, I thought about some of the field trips she took with school and church groups. There was a sweet, somewhat shy schoolmate that few befriended, especially on field trips. Wendy always made a point to ask if she could share a seat with her on the bus. Another classmate, now with grown children of his own, recently told me something about Wendy that I did not know. He said when he moved here from another state, Wendy was the only student at LCA who greeted him, and helped him find his way around the school. I was not surprised.

Wendy attended Lynchburg Christian Academy through the ninth grade before transferring to Jefferson Forest High School. She had friends in both schools. She thought she could make a difference in a public school. Dave Adams, Wendy's youth pastor, felt her spiritual strength could be a Godly influence. It didn't take long at the new school for Wendy to join many activities, including varsity cheerleading. She and a couple of church youth leaders started a Christian youth program at the school with 40 students attending. She was certainly not shy about sharing Jesus with those who didn't know Him.

Wendy continued with her church activities, including traveling and singing with The Young Believers. Showing English seat riding was a huge highlight for her. She placed high and won many ribbons for her equestrian skill in these events. Doc, our neighbor on the farm behind us, taught Wendy to ride, beginning at seven years old. I was always nervous about those high jumps, but not Wendy. She was very confident in all aspects of the sport.

My memories faded as the nurse entered the room, and she said we could spend some time with Wendy now. I was so frightened of what I might see. Harvey had to pull me literally down the hall. We entered the room hearing nothing but a loud, clicking machine which was hooked up to Wendy's lungs. The nurse told us that the machine was breathing for her. "Oh my! Oh my!" kept coming out of my mouth. I was stunned and speechless when I approached her bedside. Blood was still seeping from her nose, and the only movement in her body was that machine making her chest move up and down as it released air into her lungs. Her face was beginning to swell more, distorting the looks of our beautiful daughter. I

WHY GOD WHY?

held her hand and talked to her as if she could hear me, and maybe she did. Desperately trying to hold onto my little girl's life, I pleaded with the staff, "PLEASE don't unplug the machines!" My dearest Harvey had to hold back his feelings to comfort me during this horrible time.

We all prayed and cried together as evening fell. Then, the sight of the doctor opening the door gave way to dreadful silence. His face looked anguished and tears formed in his eyes, as those fearful words flowed from his mouth; "I am so sorry, Wendy did not make it." In shock, I jumped to my feet and yelled, "No, you promised not to unplug the machine!" "No! No!" I kept yelling. More tears swelled in his eyes as he explained that Wendy's heart just could not take any more. With shock and disbelief, I fell to the sofa. Everyone was crying and trying so hard to comfort us. We did not believe this finality would become a reality.

Wendy, just before she went to heaven

I don't know the dosage of the prescription given me, but it made me disoriented. I don't even remember the ride home or seeing Tim before we left the hospital. Later, Harvey told me that we went by to check on him and let him know we would be back. Dr. Jerry Falwell Sr., our pastor, arrived at the hospital and saw Tim shortly after we left.

I do remember my mother and Harvey putting me to bed with a wet face cloth on my head. Harvey went back to the hospital to stay with Tim while

1: *God, Please Don't Take My Children*

family and friends stayed with me to give comfort. Each time I awakened, my heart would break anew, and my moans penetrated the house as I yelled for Tim and grieved over Wendy. My mother continued to caress me and remind me that Wendy is in the arms of the Lord, and Tim will be okay. In the past, this would have helped the hurt; however, this pain was too deep. Only Jesus could help.

The next few days seemed like I was floating in a complete nightmare. I don't know what we would have done without our Lord, family, and friends. My dear Harvey made most of the funeral arrangements, including picking out a casket for our daughter. He also retrieved Tim from the hospital and brought him by to see me before taking him down the road to his parent's house for the night. Everyone was trying to spare Tim from so much grief and to give us time to pull things together; however, I wish he had been there to grieve and share this part of life's sorrow with us. Selfishly, I think I would have felt better if I had him to cuddle and hug during that time. My heart yearned for him. I suppose family thought they were protecting Tim from all the grief and pain. However, I wanted to be with our young son, and now our only child.

The deep despair and emptiness began to take a toll as I sat slumped in a chair in the living room. I was about to scream and cry when I heard a powerful familiar voice coming from the kitchen. As usual, Dr. Falwell was speaking to everyone and patting some on the back. As he came to the living room and approached my chair, I trembled when I tried to speak, "Oh, Jerry." He was one of the most uplifting, loving souls I had ever met. He took my hand and prayed with sincerity and love. Jerry had a distinct voice that I'm sure reached God faster than others. I sensed our spirits connecting with the divine power of the Holy Spirit. He was speaking through Jerry to help ease my pain. Dr. Falwell left in the same manner as he came. He made everyone feel comforted and loved, whether he was joking with them, hitting them on the arm, or just asking them about their families.

WHY GOD WHY?

So many caring people came to family night to express their love. I had cried until my tears dried up. I held on to Tim as if he was going away. Harvey had placed Wendy's karate belt and a couple of other meaningful items in the casket. Even though she had so many things on her plate, she finished that karate class for her dad, who insisted on completing whatever you start.

Wendy had many friends from both the Christian Academy and Jefferson Forest High School, so many in fact, there were over 2,000 people in attendance for the funeral. The day before the funeral, Dave Adams, Wendy's beloved youth pastor, found Wendy's diary in her room. I had not read it before, but Dave took the liberty to do so himself. Without knowing her destiny, Wendy had written her eulogy. Tears flowed as Dave read the pages. His heart was broken along with ours. He started on the page with Wendy's sixteenth birthday:

- *August 20:* It is my sixteenth birthday, and I am being grounded. I don't have a good attitude about being grounded this long and I am beginning not to be sorry anymore. Besides, I didn't do anything that bad. Oh well, for my sake and others, I will try to do better. Happy birthday to me… hum, hum…I will talk with you later Diary.

- *August 21:* I am so excited! My parents are going to let me go to Treasure Island (the church youth camp) next week.

- *August 29:* Today I went to the Island and got in the cabin with Debbie Ott (sweet). Dave introduced me to Byron, the Young Believer's (singing group) leader. We all sat around and talked, and it was great. Dean Dobson spoke tonight on being a plastic Christian—"Desire Christ and you will find Him." He is a great preacher and dean of Liberty University.

- *August 30:* I was so convicted and had to leave the service. Debbie talked with me, and it really helped. I had accepted Christ when I was a young girl, but tonight I felt like the Lord wanted more of my life. I made a list of what I would gain and lose by making the commitment to surrender my whole life to the Lord and to His service. I made that commitment and also made the Young Believers singing group.

- *August 31:* We went to the main church in town then came back to the Island. Young Believers sang in the service tonight. Message was on '17 Reasons Why Christians are Superior, Not inferior.' Greg, a few kids and I went to the chapel, and I played piano as they sang my favorite, "'I'll Rise Again."

- *September 1:* Dear Diary, this was the last day at camp. At Young Believer's practice, we became a big family unit. We love each other to death. I got to know Robin and Mark Vissers ... super people. Young Believers sang in 7:00 service and I was happy to sing with them. As Dave was preaching tonight, he told everyone that I was a blessing to him. My heart was joyful as I shared the commitment I had made, Diary. Dave said, "The trials here are nothing compared to the triumphs of heaven." He had everyone praying for me as I go back to Jefferson Forest High. What will hurt me most is if my close friends, Michael and Kathy turn me away for the life commitment I made. I wish I could tell them how much I love them. But, if they care for me as they say, then that won't happen.

- *September 2:* I know God will be with me and I have so many super sincere kids in the group praying for me. School

WHY GOD WHY?

started ... like my classes. Well, so far I see that Michael and Kathy aren't going to shut me out for the commitment. They are both sincere friends. I have the busiest schedule ... school, cheerleading practice till 6:00, karate from 7:00-8:00 and homework. But, I love it. We have a game Friday, and we've been practicing hard.

- *September 3:* Boy, today was tight. I was so pooped I thought I would faint. Girls' volleyball lost their scrimmage and Kathy had a cow as usual. I messed up at cheerleading practice today, but that is fine. I think tonight was the hardest we've had. This wouldn't have been so bad if I had been more positive. Everything will be fine. I will make A's on my tests Thursday and Friday.

That was the last page written by Wendy. She did make all A's and was happy with her accomplishments and her spiritual commitment.

Dr. Falwell and Dave delivered the message at the funeral. Dave had borrowed the diary and gave Wendy's eulogy relating her own words. For a long time, he

The last photo taken of Wendy, 16

had felt that Wendy would be used for the Lord's purpose but could never know what the Lord had in mind. The Pantana family sent chills throughout the sanctuary when they sang Wendy's favorite song, "I'll Rise Again."

> Go ahead, drive the nails in My hands, Laugh at Me, where you stand;
>
> Go ahead, and say it isn't Me, The day will come when you will see;
>
> Cause I'll Rise Again, Ain't no power on earth can tie Me down,
>
> Yes, I'll Rise Again, Death can't keep Me in the ground.
>
> Go ahead, mock My Name, My Love for you, is still the same;
>
> Go ahead, bury Me, But very soon, I will be free,
>
> Cause I'll Rise Again, Ain't no power on earth can tie Me down,
>
> Yes, I'll Rise Again, Death can't keep Me in the ground.

As Wendy would have it, Dr. Falwell laid out God's plan of salvation through Jesus Christ. Jerry gave an open invitation as he had done many times. This time seemed different. His usual, strong voice was like a chime that resonated through the sanctuary with rebound. Students from both schools began to go forward to accept as their Savior, the Jesus that Wendy knew. Fifty-five young people came forward and gave their lives to Christ.

A national youth magazine, *Telling the Truth*, got wind of Wendy's story. They featured and entitled it, 'Only One Life ... The Impact of Just One Teenager.' The captioned picture was of Wendy singing in the traveling Young Believers Ministry group. Thomas Road Baptist Church has since taken her story to youth rallies around the country, and many have accepted Christ as Savior. Pastor Dave kept Wendy's picture on his desk

WHY GOD WHY?

to remind him of this one, chosen by God. Later he told us that the impact of her life and death had changed his life and his family's in many ways.

For the next couple of weeks, I could feel Wendy's spirit throughout the house. At the end of the second week, that feeling of her actual presence left me. Shock, denial, and emptiness came over me. Reality jerked my soul, as I yelled and cried out to God. Harvey came running up from the basement when he heard me crying. I knew that Wendy was with Jesus; however, it still hurt deeply to be separated from her, and not able to soothe her. The Bible says, "To be absent from the body is to be present with the Lord." I knew Wendy didn't miss a heartbeat before entering into the presence of her Lord. I knew her spirit was gone that day, as she took her place in the glorious heaven above. We realized that Wendy's sweet spirit did not leave our hearts, and her memories would always dwell deep within us. I remember one Sunday driving home from church. Wendy was singing and full of the spirit when she confessed, "Mom, I am ready to be used for the Lord, in any way He needs me." Her comment reflected the faith she always had.

I went to the grave and poured out my heart to God, begging for strength to accept His will. I could see the Bible verse so clearly like it was written in the sky, "I will never leave you, nor forsake you. I will walk with you every step of the way, and I will never put on you more than you can bear." I began to sing one of my favorite songs, "In the Valley He Restoreth My Soul."

I went through the phase of memorializing Wendy with many pictures on the wall and many conversations about her. It just seemed to keep her close if I saw her and talked about her. A friend reminded me that Wendy was gone and that I have a son who needs me. The thought had never crossed my mind, that I was hurting my son and it broke my heart. The next few days, I spent many hours with the Lord. I talked, prayed, cried and laughed. He made it clear that I didn't need pictures all over the house to remember Wendy. She had a permanent residence in my heart. Wendy's high school picture hangs on the wall with other family pictures; all others have been put in storage.

After a dark season of lingering in the valley and questioning God, we finally surrendered ourselves to His authority. As our faith and relationship with the Lord grew, He gave us inner peace and the comfort of knowing that our valley experience was a gateway to His purpose. We continue to thank God for choosing our daughter, through life and death, to increase His Kingdom and glorify His name.

Chapter 2
PREDESTINED SOUL MATES

Harvey and I had been married eighteen years when we lost Wendy. It is hard to believe we recently celebrated our fiftieth anniversary. It seems such a short time ago that we met and started our journey together.

I was unaware of and had no control over a magical love that was about to begin in my life. I paid no attention to this scrawny boy in my department at church named Harvey. However, I was to find out a few years later, that I was on his mind during our youth years, which spilled over to the teen years. Harvey admitted to admiring me from a distance but was too embarrassed to approach me. He even followed my friends and me from church to the corner drugstore on Sunday mornings. He also joined the church youth choir so he could see me, not because he wanted to sing. Believe it or not, we were baptized the very same day. Although Harvey's home was miles across town, he would visit his uncle, who lived near my home in hopes of seeing me strolling down Rivermont Avenue. "Wow!" I surmised. You never know who and when someone is secretly watching from a distance. My friends and I wore out many pairs of shoes walking the Avenue, whether to church, school, corner drugstore or the local swimming pool. I began to wonder about Harvey, when he informed me, that in those early years of fascination toward me, God made it known to him that our future would be together.

WHY GOD WHY?

During those years, I didn't notice Harvey's attraction to me. He pointed out that I was a stuck-up young lady. I never thought of myself as being stuck-up. However, a few months before my sixteenth birthday, the tables slightly turned. I received a phone call from a boy addressing himself as Joe, a friend, and neighbor of Harvey Hamilton. "Harvey would like you to come to the 'hop' (dance) at the high school Friday night. He will be playing the guitar with this band called the Dazzlers." I explained that my mother would probably not let me go. The only dance I was ever allowed to attend was at the local playground, escorted by parents. However, I did respond with a confident tone, "I'll try to persuade her."

After many discussions, and consistent begging, mother reluctantly gave in to my request to attend the dance. Her change of heart was because my friend, Pat had coerced her father into driving us and chaperoning. Mr. Rucker was the local fire chief and well respected in the community. I'm sure my mother gave him strict orders to keep us in his sight at all times. Who would have guessed that he would strut across the gym, and climb the bleachers to get a birds-eye view of the two of us at all times?

Since I didn't know Harvey that well, I was more thrilled about going to this big sock-hop with so many other young people. Excitement filled the house as the anticipated day finally arrived. I dressed in my navy-blue skirt, a matching sailor shirt and saddle oxfords. Butterfly's in my stomach stirred, given I had never attended one of these dances before.

As we entered the huge gym, we were amazed to see so many kids dancing. Some were standing in front of the stage screaming over the band and moving their bodies to the rhythm of the music. The noise from the band with the kids screaming was rousing. To tell the truth, it was a little scary to me.

My friend, Pat and I finally gained enough nerve to walk over to the stage and get a glimpse of the one who had instigated this whole thing. Looking up, I saw an attractive young hunk I had never really noticed before. This time, my attention was completely focused on him. Harvey finally caught my eye. Then he grinned and winked, in that order. "Wow!" I thought as I saw this fifteen-year-old star with big brown eyes, and a captivating smile to boot. Honestly, I couldn't have been more flattered if Elvis himself was on the stage. Why did I ignore this cute, talented guy all these years?"

What took place next was shocking. The band took their first break and my eyes followed as Harvey slowly descended to the floor level and headed in my direction. He greeted me with the charm and grace of a true gentleman. Within a minute, a young teenybopper ran up and grabbed Harvey's hand as if she owned him. I was stunned when he introduced her as his girlfriend. He must not have been too serious about this girl because that very night he gave her walking papers and started a loving relationship with me. His dreams had come true, and I saw a love I never knew.

We were a brand new couple getting to know each other. On our third date, Harvey and I were riding in the back of a friend's car while he drove to pick up his date. Discovering that Harvey and I had never kissed got Allen's mental gears moving. He coaxed us to kiss one another. "It's your third date, man, give her a kiss," Allen teased. I could tell that Harvey wanted it to be on his timing, but he kissed me nonetheless.

We dated on a steady basis and committed ourselves to one another. Harvey hosted a sixteenth birthday party for me in his parent's basement. The next weekend, on my actual birthday, my mother agreed to let me go to the school hop and have a pajama party with several friends. Unfortunately, I contracted red measles, and my mother wouldn't permit me to go, but she did agree to the sleepover. The girls went to the dance before coming over, and I sat home sobbing because I missed watching Harvey and the band. Measles or not, we snuck out late that night, walked six blocks to the Avenue and straddled the white line in our baby-doll pajamas.

WHY GOD WHY?

During the next couple of years, I was very busy with school, band, and other activities. I was always so proud to walk the halls with Harvey. I was permitted to go out with Harvey on his gig on Saturday nights. Dating during school nights was taboo. We met at church on Sunday and sometimes strolled through Riverside Park in the afternoon. School hours were busy without much time to have social meetings. When he wasn't playing in the band on the weekends, we would cruise our favorite, short-order drive-in hangouts. Hollins Mill was my very favorite. Those were the days when you pushed a button, ordered your food and a waitress delivered it to your car on a tray that attached to the car window. That's where we saw many of our friends, drank cokes and ate French fries on the hood of the car. Like many silly girls, I would only eat one or two fries in front of my date. However, when I arrived home, I was starved, and I raided the refrigerator for leftovers.

1960, Harvey & Violet at E.C. Glass

I honestly believed our relationship was a God thing. The love between Harvey and me grew, as we dated steadily over a two-year span. One evening he asked if we could have a talk. He became logical and politically correct on me. He told me how much he respected and loved me. Then

2: *Predestined Soul Mates*

he began to remind me how young we were, and how he did not want to violate any moral standards that would harm me or that would be regretful to us both. I listened and wondered where this was going. "We have two more years of high school and then college," he said, "years that should be lived to the fullest." My heart broke when he suggested we break off our steady relationship. He went on to say that we should be free to enjoy our different activities and friendships. I questioned why, thinking we could stay together forever. It didn't make sense to me. He brought up our binding covenant and said, "you are to be my future bride, and nothing will change that. God planned our future, therefore, don't get serious with another guy." Harvey planned our marriage date would be in 1965 after all our school commitments were complete. Then he said, "I might date others, but never wish to marry anyone except my sweet Violet."

I will never forget the time Harvey thought I might be getting too serious about another guy. He reminded me of our future and took the fellow I was dating out for a little chat. Harvey told him that I was his future wife and the love of his life. There was no more to say about that. Harvey and I continued to see each other occasionally and dated others along the way. The two of us attended our prom together. The evening was all I expected ... wonderful.

Harvey was a member of the Civil Air Patrol and always had a great desire to fly airplanes. He flew several trips with the team and directors, sometimes staying at another airbase for a week at a time. Quite a bit of aircraft knowledge filled his head, and he wanted to learn more. His decision to join the Air Force, and further his education, was not surprising to me. I had applied to the school of nursing, but my heart was leaning towards being a dental hygienist. After my tour, and official meeting at the hospital, I learned that the school did not allow students to marry during their years of study and professional training. Knowing that Harvey and I had plans for marriage, I switched my vocation.

WHY GOD WHY?

We were married, June 8, 1963, two years earlier than Harvey's original marital plans. The joy of being married in our church, where we first met, added to the wonderful occasion. He was home on a thirty-day leave from Denver, Colorado. The thought of putting a wedding together in thirty days aged my mother. However, everything totally worked out. The company my mother chose to print the invitations scheduled us as a top priority. A local bridal shop had the perfect dress for me, as well as coordinate dresses for my sisters Jan and Sheilla, my friend Linda, and Harvey's sister, Pat who were my attendants. Our only mishap was receiving the wrong bouquets of flowers for the attendants. At the last hour before the wedding, we sent them back to the florist and retrieved the correct ones.

There was more crying going on during our wedding than was customary. The young girl, whom I babysat for years, started to cry. Then my mother and grandmother began to cry, along with a couple of old girlfriends of Harvey's. With so much crying going on behind me, I started to cry. These were all tears of joy. The minister stopped long enough to remind me that this was a joyous event and he handed me his hanky. It seemed everyone was crying out of happiness for a couple who loved each other for so long.

After a short honeymoon, Harvey returned to his school and commitment in Denver. I missed him terribly, but in three months he was transferred to Massachusetts where I joined him by way of a train. My mother and mother-in-law gave me plenty of traveling advice at the train station: "Don't talk to any strangers and hold your pocketbook tightly under your arm." I think they scared me more than advised me. They went so far as to explain their safety concerns for me to the conductor. I was embarrassed. Their next advice shocked me—how not to start a family too early in the marriage. The problem was, they both had completely different instructions for me.

2: *Predestined Soul Mates*

Strutting in my green skirt, vest, matching beret and heels, I proudly boarded the train. The conductor did check on me several times, while I stayed glued to my seat. I managed to find a lady's room but hurried back to my seat as if someone was going to take it. After I had calmed down, the conductor took me on a tour through a few of the cars. One had a casket housing a soldier's body.

Finally, after so many hours, the conductor announced our arrival into the Springfield station. I wanted to look my best for Harvey, but was a little disheveled by the time I arrived. Nonetheless, all was perfect when I stepped off the train and saw him smiling with delight. We were so thrilled to be together again.

God had ordained our marriage and was walking us through the first year of our journey.

Chapter 3
WHAT FAIRYTALE LIFE?

We all have expectations of the first-year of our marriage. We envision a fairytale is going to come true. We dream about the white picket fence, the ocean on one side, mountains on the other and candle-lit dinners. That was my mental picture. Living my life with Harvey was all I needed, regardless of what and where.

I had never, previously, traveled so far from my hometown and family. Massachusetts seemed like another continent. It was cold with heavy snow. Nothing like I had ever seen in Virginia. Harvey and I lived in a small trailer twenty-five miles from the Air Force base. We only had one car, and Harvey used it for work each day. That was a little scary for me. Some nights he practiced with a band, with whom he played guitar. Most of their engagements were on the weekends.

Our home had very tiny rooms, and that took some adjusting on my part. I had to go outside to dust-mop under our bed and even worse, I practically had to enter the bathroom assuming the position. Well, not quite that bad. The guestroom had a walk-thru to our bedroom. The sitting room sofa had a skirt on the bottom that looked out of place. I was amazed to later discover it had no legs and was held up by full antifreeze cans. Regardless, I dearly loved our first little home.

Harvey introduced me to New York style pizza, grinders (huge subs) and McDonald's burgers. Previously, the only pizza I knew was the one

WHY GOD WHY?

my mother put together from a box. Harvey had experienced some of those delicacies while traveling with the military. I'm not sure what he expected from my cooking, or non-cooking. I knew how to cook eggs, make gravy, toast bread and boil corn. Trying other things, like burnt beans and half cooked spaghetti didn't help my self-esteem. Harvey didn't fret; he just wanted me there, cooking or not.

I knew cooking wasn't my thing, but I thought washing clothes should be a cinch. There was a coin-operated laundromat on the premises. The washers looked like something from outer space, with money arms attached. I decided my first load would be a practice run, but I overfilled the washing machine with detergent. There could be no practice run for the first dryer load. The temperature of the dryer was so hot that it disintegrated my new negligee. It melted. Standing there with the pieces in my hand and my mouth wide open in shock, a young fellow inquired into my problem. Here I was, a grown woman being taught how to dry clothes by a young fellow. That was embarrassing, to say the least. All I could think of was I hoped he doesn't tell his mother.

I knew my mother always had a bottle of Clorox but wasn't sure how to use it. I opened the top and took a big sniff, which almost made me pass out. There was no way that smell was going on my clothes. To add salt to my wounds, I placed that bottle of Clorox on the guestroom bed. Picking it up a few days later, I discovered the top was not on properly, and the leak had eaten a hole in the bedspread. They say we learn from our mistakes. I certainly learned my share in one week's time.

Harvey worked long hours at the base, practiced with the band some evenings, and played music on weekends. I was so lonesome for him and yearned for a friend. However, getting to know the neighbors and making new friends was just not going to happen. There was no over-the-fence chatting among people in the neighborhood. Everyone kept to themselves. When they drove by I would wave to them, but received few gestures in return. Having always gone to church, I was sure we would find many friends there. Being a little naïve, I thought all churches were full of friendly welcoming members. To my dismay, there were no warm, fuzzy feelings there either. Later on, however, we did discover a uniqueness about our Northern friends. When they became your friend, they were dedicated, caring friends. Several months later, one couple took us under their wings as if we were their children. By that time, I probably looked like a little-lost sheep needing some tending. Harvey's band was getting more and more requests to play leaving me with many sad and frightened nights. Occasionally I would accompany Harvey if the place was proper for me.

One evening when I was alone I started watching a Billy Graham Crusade on television. He asked a direct question; "If you were to die tonight, do you know where you would spend eternity, heaven or hell? The Bible says there is only one way to enter heaven. The phone rang, and I did not hear that 'one way' part of his sermon. I thought about what he said and had unsettled convictions about my eternal life. I could not say for sure that I was bound for heaven. I was not accustomed to being alone at night, especially with no neighbor friends. I cried, "Mama, how I wish you were here." These were the times I really longed for and appreciated home.

The next morning was a new day to rejoice and be glad in it. I was encouraging myself to think positively. Harvey was working at the base, and I was cleaning house with the TV blaring. Suddenly an emergency news break came on. The newsman seemed filled with emotion, and it brought my attention to the television. The announcement to our nation and the world was shocking and unbelievable. "American people, our President has been assassinated," came from the announcer's shaky voice. "Yes, John F. Kennedy has been shot by an assassin's bullet while riding with his wife in the Dallas parade!" The emotion shown from the

WHY GOD WHY?

announcer's voice was fright, concern, and sadness. Over and over, they broadcasted this heartbreaking news. My neighbors, whom I did not know, began to run into the streets yelling and crying in panic mode. Small children were holding onto their mom's skirts in fright. Massachusetts was the home of President Kennedy; they did not take the news lightly, nor did anyone in the nation. We were all stunned and frightened.

Soon the footage of that awful moment filled our homes and hearts with pain and despair. The President had fallen over in the lap of the First Lady, Jackie Kennedy. Our hearts broke as we felt the impact of the President's death. Fear and insecurity filled the hearts of the people of our country. Our nation was in a vulnerable state. The unknown, upcoming days moved the American people to pull together and seek spiritual help through unity prayer. It was a time to hold close to family and pray together.

Christmas was just around the corner. The thought of not seeing my family weighed heavy on my heart. One thing I wanted was a Christmas tree, small home or not. My desire for a Christmas tree did not interest Harvey. "Honey," I projected; "we are going to celebrate this glorious time with traditional family customs, including a tree and a manger." Harvey finally drove me to a tree lot where I looked for a tree small enough to fit in our little den. It never crossed our minds to buy a stand for the tree; however, I did find a bucket that would do the job nicely. Filling the bucket with dirt using a spoon was a challenge. Also, there was only one place not covered with two feet of snow. Here I was, halfway under our trailer with my feet sticking out above the snow. It took a while to fill the bucket using a serving spoon to dig with. My body was frozen, and it was a lot more difficult to exit than it was to enter. I was hoping the next-door neighbors didn't witness this crazy sight. With the help of a few rocks, the bucket worked nicely.

I cut a manger scene from a book and taped it to a shoebox. Not having real figures, did not upset me. My mother taught us how to improvise.

3: What Fairytale Life?

Harvey & our first Christmas tree in Massachusetts

Except for a small box of Christmas balls and tinsel, our tree was trimmed with popcorn and cut out stars. Once the presents arrived from home, and I placed them under the little tree it looked more festive.

Christmas morning was exciting for me. It was the first Christmas that I didn't pre-peak into the presents, as I did back home. Harvey set up the automatic camera to capture us on our first Christmas morning together. We laugh when we look back at those pictures of that scrawny little tree and the two of us half asleep, sitting on the sofa in our PJs.

The holidays had passed, and things settled down for the New Year. For a few days, I wasn't feeling well and began to worry about my health. I made an appointment with a doctor on the Air Force base. By the time of my appointment, I was so very sick. Naïve as I was about things, I did not understand why the doctor was laughing after I disclosed my symptoms to him. "Mrs. Hamilton, I don't even have to test you to identify your problem. You are going to have a baby!" You could have knocked me over with a feather.

We had only been married for seven months. Very few times have I been speechless, but this was one of those times. I had a terrible feeling deep inside because Harvey expressed his negative thoughts of having a baby so early in our marriage. I felt so alone when all I wanted was for him to give me a big hug and express his happiness. Harvey's good friend and mentor expressed his dissatisfaction with Harvey's attitude. "You should be thankful and praise God for this blessed gift," he reprimanded. Harvey took it to heart and began thanking God.

Directions from the doctor were clear but questionable. A urine specimen was to be dropped off at the hospital lab during the next few days. I didn't know anything about collecting a urine specimen because my mother always handled those things. The doctor's office didn't give me anything in which to collect it in, and all I could find in the house was an empty pickle jar, and it didn't have a lid. "Reynolds-wrap and a rubber band will be okay," I figured. My next question was, "How much specimen will they need for the test?" Oh yes, I filled half of that jar, capped it with the Reynolds-wrap and a rubber band, and placed it in a paper bag. If my mother had any knowledge of this, she would have disowned me. Well, she shouldn't have done everything for me. How would I know what to do? She probably did tell me things like this, but I paid no attention. I depended on her for so many things.

Grinning proudly, I walked into the lab with my brown bag. There were many military men lined up waiting at the receiving desk. When it was my turn, I reached into the bag and pulled out my pickle jar, and placed it on the counter. The airmen were staring at me so strangely. To top that, I looked at the guy behind the desk and asked, "Can you tell if it's positive by looking?" There was snickering in the background. If Harvey had gone in with me, he would have turned three shades of red. And so it was, we were going to be parents.

"Give thanks and praise God for this blessing." That was the advice that we held dearly during the next few months.

Chapter 4
TRANSFORMATION AND CREATION

I was almost three months pregnant when Harvey got his orders to relocate to Bossier City, Louisiana, just outside of Shreveport. He had a 15-day leave so we could visit our hometown on the way down south. Being an expectant mother made this trip long and tiring. Arriving a few miles from our destination, I was dazzled by the hundreds of colorful, flashing signs and marquee lights that lasted for blocks. "This is called 'The Strip,' where celebrity country singers perform," said Harvey.

"Honey, I am completely famished," I moaned as we entered Bossier City. We pulled into a drive-in and ordered hotdogs and cokes. I was told many funny things about down south, but I had never seen anyone slice up a hot dog and place it on a hamburger bun. Starvation won over my determination not to eat a hotdog on a hamburger bun. Unusual or not, I gobbled it down and was satisfied for the night. We finally found our little house in the middle of Bossier City suburbia. Thank goodness the house was furnished, because we had no furniture.

We attended the Bossier City Baptist church on our first Sunday, March 13, 1964. Several couples from the Air Force base also attended this church. That same afternoon, the pastor and music director visited our home and welcomed us to their church and the area. After a few minutes of introductions, the pastor asked us an unsettling question; "Are you folks saved," and "Do you know Jesus as your personal Savior?" I was not familiar with the term—saved. I replied, "We belong to a Baptist church in Lynchburg, Virginia. "That's good," he said, "but, are you folks saved?" Not knowing exactly the answer he was looking for, I replied, "We were baptized when we were eleven." Persistence must have been his middle name, as he asked the third time with a different question, "If you folks died today, do you know where you would spend eternity?" By that time, I was a little irritated and just blurted out, "Yes!" Deep in my heart, I was not sure I knew the answer to that question. Harvey just sat and listened.

My conscience and curiosity led us back to that church for the night service. I was still under great conviction from hearing Billy Graham and had to find answers. We settled into a distant pew to listen to this same, short, spunky pastor, with a booming voice preach as I had never heard the Gospel preached before. He talked about God's love and His gift of salvation. As he quoted Scripture, I began to see the light, "For by grace are you saved, through faith; and that not of yourselves; it is the gift of God; not of works, lest any man should boast." The pastor became silent, then said, "God's gift to you is free. All you need to do is receive it, by believing that Jesus Christ died for you on the cross, taking all of your sins (past, present, future) on Himself. He also rose from the grave the third day, giving you victory over the grave. If you want to be a child of God and be assured of your place in heaven, invite Jesus into your heart, as the Savior of your life, right now. Bow your heads and tell the Lord that you know you are a sinner, and that you want to put your faith and trust in Him (Jesus), who took those sins on the cross. Ask Him to forgive you of your sins and save you for eternity in heaven with Him." I won't forget what he said at the end, "The last thing that you may be assured of, 'God said it, so believe it. You are a child of the King and joint-heirs with Christ."

4: *Transformation & Creation*

The pastor gave an altar call for those who had given their hearts to Christ and wanted to announce it publicly by coming forward. Relief and excitement filled my soul. Feeling like someone or something was pulling me from my seat, I exited the pew and ran down the aisle to profess that I had opened my heart to Jesus as Savior of my life. Right there, the pastor prayed with me. Burdens were lifted that night, and I began a personal relationship with the Lord Jesus Christ. Harvey did not accept Christ as his Savior until we returned home a couple of years later.

Our first week in Louisiana was not without excitement. I knew that this part of the country could have some terrible storms. However, I did not expect to experience my first tornado so quickly, or at all. Watching the devastation of this storm on TV, frightened me to death. I tried to reach Harvey at the base, only to find that the phone lines were down. Tree limbs were blowing against the house as if they were sticks. Pouring down rain and hail blocked my vision outside. Holding my stomach with little Wendy inside, I bundled up on the sofa and prayed for our safety. Suddenly, almost as quickly as it came, the storm blew over. I was amazed to see a cow right outside our front window. "There are no cows around this neighborhood; did the wind blow it here?" I wondered. Immediately after the storm, Harvey rushed home to check on me. I was thrilled to see him.

The months passed quickly and my time was getting closer to the delivery date. My mother was very concerned for me and sent my sister, Jan for support. Her back was hurting so badly from the very long bus trip that she could hardly stand up straight. Nonetheless, it was wonderful having her with me. She didn't like the Louisiana heat at all. It is a different type of heat in Louisiana than Virginia and takes some time to adjust to it.

God blessed us with our first bundle of joy, Wendy Faith Hamilton on August 20, 1964. I was frightened and wished my mother could have been there to comfort me. The nurses helped while I was in the hospital, but when it was time to leave, they handed me the little package of joy and wished me good luck. Taking on the responsibility of a living baby is a scary thought, and we had many things to learn along the way. I made numerous, inquiring, phone calls to my mother for her advice. Friends from church visited and brought several dishes of wonderful southern foods.

The joy of having Wendy in our lives far outweighed the parental responsibility. Harvey and I had been juggling work, college studies, and church commitments. I took a sabbatical from everything except being a wife and mother along with a couple of church activities. We both became active in church and enjoyed our new Christian friends.

Harvey had a military leave coming up, and we were excited to travel home with our Wendy, who was three months old. When we arrived, all of the family members were waiting with outstretched arms. We were grateful that we had the opportunity to share time with both families.

One night, when everyone was relaxing and playing in the basement, I started down the steps with Wendy to join in the fun. She was cradled in my arms, but I slipped and fell down the flight of stairs. Although my arms cushioned her when I fell, I was an emotional wreck. It tore me all to pieces to think of what could have happened.

A few days later, Harvey's grandfather passed away. Everyone had to divide their time between Wendy and the funeral events. Many distant family members who were there for the funeral were able to enjoy time with us and our new baby girl.

It was time for us to travel back to Louisiana far too soon. Goodbyes were so very hard this time. The family sent us with prayers of safety. Going back was not as exciting for us. In fact, it seemed so much longer and harder.

Wendy's first birthday party was as thrilling for me as much as it was for her. The neighborhood children played and cared for her. During one of the games around the yard, all the girls began to scream. I turned around to see the ugliest creature I had ever seen. It looked like a possum with a hard shell on its back. The other parents were laughing. They were surprised that I had never seen an armadillo before. "No," I said, "and I don't want to see any more of them."

We took many pictures to send back home of her birthday party. Little Wendy had such a good time with all her little playmates. I had never seen any child as excited as she was to rip into those gifts wrapped with beautiful paper and balloons. That's what it is all about—the joy and happiness.

Military days were finally coming to an end. The anticipation of moving back home kept my spirits high. Wendy was sixteen months old when we were going to return home. She was the perfect age for grandparents to enjoy and spoil. This time, the trip seemed shorter. We were finally headed home to stay. Praise the Lord!

1965, The Hamilton Family:
Violet, Wendy & Harvey

Chapter 5
THE ABANDONED WELL

As I remembered that this day was the anniversary of Wendy's new life in heaven, a ride through the countryside helped me realize the splendor of her surroundings. When I was alone, my mind usually lingered on events and times with Wendy. I recalled the first test of her faith. It took place just before her seventh birthday.

Many times on the weekends we visited my mom and stepfather. However, this particular one added a few years to my life. I drove to my mother's house, with Wendy and my niece, Cindy, who was staying with us for the weekend. They were close cousins and got together every time they could. Harvey was about 50 miles away on a music gig, and my stepfather was away on business, so we had a girl's day.

Wendy asked if they could play with my mother's longtime neighbor Pat's children for a while. Pat was delighted for the girls to play together. Meanwhile, my mom and I sat lethargically on the porch, drinking tea and admiring the beauty of the afternoon. We chatted away, bringing each other up-to-date on the latest news, and laughing about the good old times. Suddenly, we heard a terrifying scream from a child in the distance. My mother and I jumped to our feet. Little Cindy was running as fast as her legs would carry her and screaming in horror, "Wendy fell into a well, and we can't see her!" I couldn't believe my ears as I tried calming her to make sure I heard her correctly. As she began to repeat her words, my

WHY GOD WHY?

knees weakened, and I frantically looked at my mother. We both ran to Pat's backyard, where the children had been playing.

Pat and her neighbor, Frank, were looking down into a cement well that protruded out of the ground about twenty-five inches. Pat confirmed Cindy's frightening words, "Wendy just disappeared, plunging down into this old well. We haven't used it for years except to throw discarded items down into it." My heart was pounding out of control as I listened to Pat's trembling voice. She added that they could not see Wendy, even with a flashlight, but they could hear her faint voice far down into the ground.

I discovered from the children that they were playing on an old porch swing that had been put on top of the well. It suddenly broke in half, and everyone cleared the hole but Wendy. She and the swing went down the well together.

I took my mother's hand, and together we walked over to the well. I could only see down about twenty-five feet into this dark hole, and Wendy was not in sight. Leaning over the small opening, I yelled to her. I finally heard her faint little voice, seemingly miles away echoing from the well, "Mama, I'm down here, and I can't stand on this pipe much longer. I'm afraid I'm going to fall!" "Oh my, how far down is she?" I thought. My mind started playing tricks on me, wondering if the well had water or even snakes. Panic stricken, I turned to my mother who was in shock herself.

Pat went into her house to call the fire and rescue squads for help. Frank had retrieved a 35-foot rope from his shed; then he dropped the rope down the well. I yelled loudly, "Wendy honey, can you grab the rope and pull yourself up?" Wendy's sad little voice echoed back, "Mama, the rope didn't come down here." I desperately looked to Frank for answers, "Where is she?" I asked. He was not short on words as he remembered that some of those wells were over 75 feet deep, with a pointed shaft up the center. I was about to lose it, thinking that Wendy was about to fall off

5: *The Abandoned Well*

a pipe onto this shaft, or into water. I cried out with my whole heart, "Oh God, please have mercy and help Wendy!"

A strange mental strength came over me. I knew I had to be brave for Wendy's sake and put my faith and trust in the Lord. "Hang on sweetheart, help is coming and you will be out soon," I yelled. At times it seemed that her little voice was trying to calm me. I had to put my ear directly over the hole to hear her voice, and she sounded weary and tired. She said her feet were cold and numb. I looked around screaming, "Where are the rescue trucks?" I noticed that people from all over were gathered around to pray and support us. Maybe they heard about this on the radio or their CB radios.

Over an hour had passed since Wendy fell and dusk was beginning to fall over the area. It seemed like an eternity since Pat phoned for help and my voice was getting hoarse. Nightfall was coming, and Wendy wouldn't be able to see any light from above. I closed my eyes and prayed again, "Oh God, I don't want to lose faith, but please comfort Wendy and give her the faith to know that You are there with her." Again, a calm feeling came over me, and I told Wendy that Frank was going to get a bigger light for her to see.

Finally, I could hear sirens in the distance that became louder and louder as they approached the house. "Wendy, help is here honey, and everything will be alright," I kept repeating those words in hopes of keeping her attention. A couple of fire trucks, escorted by the police, pulled right through to the backyard. I wondered how they were going to get her out of that well. Four firemen came running, bringing a very long rope ladder. They dropped the ladder in the hole and yelled for Wendy to stay put, and told her they would come down to get her. The largest fireman of them all started down the ladder to retrieve Wendy. As he climbed down this very small hole, Wendy's light must have begun to fade. He kept descending, and I thought he would never get to her. My heart was overjoyed when he

WHY GOD WHY?

spotted her with his flashlight. Before he could give her instructions, she quickly climbed through his legs and began to run up the long ladder with surprising energy. "Praise God," I shouted! I felt great relief with a heart full of thankfulness when her little head cleared the well opening.

When Wendy came out of that underground tomb, she looked like a little shaggy kitten; other than that, she seemed to be in good shape. I grabbed her up into my arms, hugged and kissed on her while expressing my love for her. The fireman said Wendy had fallen at least 45 feet. Unbelievably, we only saw one scratch on her back, and she was not complaining about other injuries. They suggested we take her to the emergency room to check for any broken bones or delayed trauma. I thanked and hugged the firemen ever so graciously for their help.

My mother and Cindy followed close behind as I carried Wendy down the street to my mom's house. No one had to say anything, the expression of joy and relief was evident on our faces. The silence broke when Wendy, very sincerely, said, "I'm glad I was the one to fall in the well because I knew the Lord was down there with me."

By this time, Harvey, his mom, and dad had received word of the accident and met us at the hospital. Doctors were amazed that Wendy had no broken bones, head injury or anything but a scratch on her back. Furthermore, they were surprised that she was in such good mental condition.

The next morning's headlines reported, "Young Girl Falls 45 Feet into a Well." We were very aware that God had sent Wendy's protective angel to keep and comfort her. Her strong faith and emotional stability were a testimony to many that day.

Chapter 6
HE PRAYED, GOD LISTENED

These were challenging times for us. Harvey was a full-time student, and also worked a full-time job.

To get our feet wet, we took on driving a church bus on Sundays for our ministry. Our route covered portions of the county that included valleys and the mountains. We had to go in one home and dress the children for church. Their mother was a third shift nurse and their father was an unreliable alcoholic.

Our bus riders included small children, teens and two elderly ladies. The children were a little rough around the edges. What they needed was attention and ears to listen to them. We discovered that a couple of the teens had deep emotional problems. One of the ladies, who lived at the highest part of the mountain needed help getting from the house to the bus. She was a senior prayer warrior who had the faith of receiving answers from God.

Our donuts and hot chocolate were the only breakfast some children had, therefore, we made sure we had plenty. Wendy loved little kids and they were excited to see her. With a big smile, Wendy, who was around nine years and growing, would serve each one as if they were royalty. There were times the bus was decorated with spilled hot chocolate.

WHY GOD WHY?

Some of the mountain roads were very scary. Some were just dirt roads, some were gravel roads, and we encountered icy bridges sometimes. Nevertheless, this was our family service to God, and to our church. We prayed and trusted God, giving Him the glory for our service and our riders.

During this time, Harvey decided he wanted to have a son, and started praying for one daily. My doctor suggested that I may not get pregnant again. That did not deter Harvey from praying as if it was to be so. Each Sunday, he had everyone on the bus praying for this boy-child that he wanted. They were excited as they prayed with the same faith as Harvey. It made them feel important and needed.

A couple of months later, those Sunday bus rides brought about some very sick mornings for me. "WOW! Could it be true, I thought to myself?" The prayers of God's faithful did get answered, and our little boy became a reality. Harvey kept the faith all along. He prayed, and God listened.

As my stomach began to grow, Wendy asked if she could help name her brother. She wanted him to have a biblical name and chose the name, Timothy. I wanted his middle name to be Scott. Wendy became excited as she counted the days, and marked off the days on the calendar.

Timothy Scott Hamilton entered this world, bellowing like a lost puppy. When they laid him on my chest, he immediately became calm and content. Looking at him, I thought; "Okay son, the Lord gave you to us, and I give you back to Him to guide you every step of the way." Harvey was beaming when the nurses brought him back to the delivery room. "Yes!" he said with confidence and certainty. "This is my son, Timothy! He was sent, straight from God," Harvey proudly announced. Ten years between siblings was a little too long. We had almost forgotten how to care for a fragile little one.

I was hospitalized for blood clots in my right lung, which had come through my heart. I was so worried that Tim would not know me. Harvey, his sister, Pat, and Wendy cared for Tim the best they knew how. Each

6: *He Prayed, God Listened*

Cindy, Wendy & Tim on his 1st birthday

night, Harvey laid in his lounge chair with Tim on his chest, as he read the Bible to him. Not only that, he allowed Tim to sleep there each and every night.

How I longed to be home with Harvey, Wendy and little Tim! I didn't get to see Tim for two weeks. When the family brought him to the hospital to see me, I thought something terrible had happened to him. He wasn't born with much hair, but the little he had was now gone. The nurse calmed my fears when she explained that babies usually lose their hair at first.

My hospital days were finally over. Everything was great, except for one thing. Tim was spoiled because he was accustomed to sleeping on Harvey's chest every night. Talk about "Waaaah!" My goodness, my precious boy had a set of lungs on him. Every couple of hours he would wake up realizing he was not lying on Dad's warm, comfortable body.

As time went by, I had heard that babies could learn to swim, so I would lay Tim on my stomach, in the tub, and lower him into the water. When he was a little older, we would take him to the lake and guide him underwater to one another. He moved like a fish and had no fear of water. Before Tim was three, he could swim the length of the pool underwater.

WHY GOD WHY?

Wendy loved Tim very much, but at times he was the classic toddler nuisance. He wanted to follow Wendy and her friends everywhere. He could figure ways to outsmart the girls, including his sister. Wendy always took care of her prize English riding attire, and kept them up and away from Tim. One morning Tim came out of her room wearing his pajamas, Mr. Potato Head glasses, Wendy's riding hat and her boots that came up to his crotch. That was one of the funniest sights we had ever seen. We all laughed till our sides hurt, including Wendy. I took a picture of him and still laugh every time I see it.

Tim liked to copy some of Wendy's habits. When she woke up, she enjoyed curling up on the floor in front of the refrigerator. She claimed that it soothed her and it put her back to sleep. Wendy often requested a dip egg (soft yolk) and toast for breakfast. I thought it was a waste to dip the yolk and leave the remainder, but of course, Tim followed suit, laying in front of the refrigerator and requested a dip egg, too!

Tim and Wendy both liked outside activities, especially when Wendy would ride him all over the farm on horseback. On one of those occasions, Wendy talked to Tim about Jesus and how He died for us. Tim knew about some of these things, but she told him who Jesus was and what He did by taking all our sins upon Himself. That day Tim asked Jesus to forgive him for all his sins and received Him into his heart as his Savior. Harvey and I rejoiced! Wendy found favor with the Lord, and now Tim had eternal life in heaven. God blessed Wendy for following His direction.

Chapter 7
WHY SUICIDE?

From the age of three, Wendy cherished horses. Her Christmas gifts always included toy horses and things associated with horses. She did very well with ballet and piano and loved sitting around our home making music with her dad, but her love for the equine world grew stronger as she grew up. Being tagged as a nature girl made this passion even more appealing.

Wendy's life changed for the better when we moved out of the city to rural America. Doc, as we respectfully referred to him, lived on the farm behind our home with his wife. He was a senior citizen and still practiced medicine. More than that, Doc owned the very thing Wendy loved—horses! The barn was just across the fence from the end of our property. She would call both horses over and pet them through the fence. She was completely unafraid of them. One day she finally gathered up enough courage to venture over to the barn. Wendy was fearless! She walked up to them and began to rub their heads. She would talk to the two of them as if she were having a conversation with human beings.

Wendy had not previously met Doc. I wasn't sure how he would take to her being around the horses. One afternoon while she was at the barn, uninvited, Doc came to take a ride. He and Wendy struck up an interesting conversation about her love for horses. Although Doc was a little on the eccentric side, he had a way with children. On the other hand, Wendy had a

WHY GOD WHY?

beautiful heart and communicated with people of all ages. Needless to say, the two of them hit it off fabulously and became good friends.

For the next couple of weeks, Wendy spent time hanging around the barn in hopes Doc would take her riding. When he finally showed up again, not only did he take her riding, he gave her a riding lesson in English seat. Wendy showed such potential that Doc agreed to continue giving her lessons. "Oh, my!" I exclaimed as she looked to be floating on cloud nine each time she rode.

The next few days, she did her chores right away and finished her homework early. She became a top hand at the stables and didn't mind being on poop control. Each evening during her prayer time, she thanked the Lord for answering her prayers.

Doc belonged to the local Hunt Club and took Wendy on the hunt a couple of times. On occasion, we would allow her to skip our church to ride with him through the back woods to his church. They would tie up the horses to a tree out back beside the cemetery. One would think they were royalty, watching the two of them mosey into church strutting their riding attire. Everyone knew the Doc, and always greeted him with love and respect. He took pride in introducing Wendy, which made her feel very special.

Other than her church activities and piano, Wendy helped with the horses whenever she could. She cleaned out the barn, fed and brushed them and brought them in for the night. Those were tasks Wendy did not mind doing. Rain, sleet, snow, day or night, she made herself available to help. Whenever she and Doc went for short rides, he would tell her about his poetry and she would tell him about the Lord.

Doc was a very special person who took advantage of all the good things life had to offer. Although he was in his early seventies, no grass grew under his feet. He still practiced medicine, was in the Hunt Club, played tennis, wrote poetry and even made his own yogurt. On occasion,

7: Why Suicide?

Wendy loved her horses and took care of them

Doc and Harvey would play tennis. Doc might have been older and a little slower, but usually played smarter and defeated Harvey.

One day we were helping Doc clean out his garage. Our son, Tim, climbed onto something he shouldn't have, and Doc took a broom and swiped him across the buttocks. I was a little stunned, but that was just Doc. He was the kind of guy who spoke his mind. Doc invited us to take advantage of his lake whenever we wanted. He warned, "Except, you better call first. I'm apt to run down for a swim in my birthday suit whenever it hits me."

Doc taught Wendy to be proficient in cantering her horse and jumping exercises. When Wendy became a teenager, we decided to buy a couple of horses of our own. She had taken riding lessons from two different schools and teachers. Wendy trained and showed her little Arabian. They were a lovely twosome together. Arabians hold their tails high, and Wendy held her back straight as they rode around the track. We quickly learned

WHY GOD WHY?

Wendy was a little upset with her Arabian, Nina when she got third place

how to braid tails and manes and even added bows. Wendy became proficient in equestrian skills. Whenever there were "Little Tykes" events, she would enter her little brother, Tim. Around the track, she guided him to the winner's circle. He was so proud of himself.

Tim would sometimes accompany Wendy to the stables to see the horses. Doc told her always to be careful with young Tim and keep her eyes on him. She had taught him how to go around the horse slowly, patting along the way. Forgetting, as little boys do, one day he ran up under the horse's head, and the horse immediately moved and stepped on Tim's foot. No bones broke, but his foot was very bruised and sore for a few days.

Life was going well for Wendy. Then came the cold, unexplained, and humbling experience that left her devastated. Phone calls started coming in, and the word was out that Doc had taken his life. Not only was this a total shock to us, but it shocked the entire community. Why suicide? We just couldn't understand why. Doc was a kind man who helped others and seemed to be happy. Wendy sobbed, "How could this happen?"

It was a cold, bitter night and snow had covered the ground. Wendy knew that two of the horses were down in the field and needed to be brought in, fed and stalled. Harvey wanted to do this task for her, but she insisted on doing it herself. I think Wendy wanted time to be alone and wanted to help Doc for the last time. With her head hung low, she slowly moved through the backyard and crossed the fence like it was her last day on earth. In the distant wind, I could hear her voice call out to the horses. Getting no response, she headed down through the fields to retrieve them. It was dusk, and it was cold and wet out. I worried about her, and yet, Wendy was never afraid of anything. Her close relationship with Jesus was always her security. I was soon relieved when I saw her riding bareback on one horse and pulling the other with the bridle, as she had done so many times before. Harvey went to the barn to comfort her as she completed her chores. He listened to her concerns for a while before heading home. She didn't exactly know where the Doc stood with Jesus, but hoped that some of her conversations had led him to receive the Lord into his heart.

It was a long, sorrowful night that spilled over into a beautiful morning which reflected a wonderful, powerful God. The same God from whom we get our strength is the same God who brought Wendy through this time of sadness. She cherished the poetry and books Doc had given her, and also held on to her memories of the friend who introduced her to horseback riding.

Chapter 8
HAVE THEY BEEN KIDNAPPED?

Wendy started attending Lynchburg Christian Academy (LCA) in kindergarten and was active all through her school years and in the youth programs at the church. We were pleased with the school and Wendy's achievements.

When Wendy was twelve years old, her longtime friend, Jackie, transferred from LCA to another Christian school in town. They had been best friends for years, and Wendy begged to move with her to this other school. My heart was with LCA, and I did not want her to leave, however, she kept insisting on changing. I don't know why I let my emotions take over my better judgment, but I agreed to let her transfer.

Everything went along just fine for the first few weeks. Wendy got along with her teachers, her grades were good, and she joined the junior school band. She was happy because her friend Jackie was there to pal around with her.

The school hired a new gym teacher, who had an unfriendly disposition and displayed a bad attitude. For some odd reason, this teacher was determined to make Wendy and Jackie's lives miserable. Wendy never had problems with teachers, before, so we couldn't understand this situ-

WHY GOD WHY?

ation. After several complaints from Wendy, we decided to approach the teacher to determine the nature of the problem. Before we could schedule an appointment, Wendy and Jackie were both verbally reprimanded, and given notes from that teacher to us. The girls decided to make a plan and acted on it.

Tim was only two years old at the time and stayed with the babysitter during the day. Usually, Wendy would get off the school bus at the sitter's, which was about a mile and a half from our house. That particular day, I arrived at the babysitter's house after work to pick up Wendy and Tim. She told me that Wendy did not get off the bus. The sitter didn't know if Wendy was even on the bus because the stop was not visible from her house. I grabbed Tim and took off for home, where I expected to find Wendy.

Wendy was not there. I assumed she must be at her favorite place, the farm next door, where she loved riding. There was no sign of her riding in the fields. I called out towards the barn and didn't get an answer. Returning to the house, I changed into suitable clothes to look for her. Entering the back door, I noticed a note on the counter. It was Wendy's handwriting, and it read, "Mom, I have run away from home. My gym teacher sent a note home, and she said things to Jackie and me that were very scary. I am scared to go back to that school." I was astonished wondering about such an action from a teacher. I thought, "Wendy never had any problems at school before."

Suddenly, my mind refocused, and I thought of every "what if" in the book. "What if Wendy went to the highway and someone picked her up? Oh Lord, what if she has been kidnapped?"

None of our neighbors had seen Wendy. I phoned Harvey and asked him to get home quickly. About that time, I received a phone call from Jackie's mother. Jackie had not come home from school, and she wondered if Wendy saw her get on her bus. Relaying the message about Wendy's note,

8: *Have They Been Kidnapped?*

we deduced that she and Jackie must be together. Jackie's mother and father came to our house to help find the girls.

Night was about to fall upon us, and I became more worried than ever. How would they find their way home in the dark of night? Or worse, what if they had been kidnapped by someone on the highway and wouldn't be coming home? "Oh Lord, please keep the girls safe wherever they are, comfort them, and let them know, You are with them," I prayed. When night set in, it brought not only the darkness but also the heaviest rainfall I had ever seen.

Family and friends came by, and we all prayed for the girls' safety. As time passed, we decided to phone the local television station in hopes that they might announce the girls were missing. The announcement rang over the airways, leading many caring people to call. Volunteers, including some of the National Guard, came to search far back into the woods, where Wendy frequently rode horses with our neighbor.

The rain was so hard that it became difficult to hike the woods or hear the girls if they called out for help. Still, they continued for hours, before the weather made it too difficult to keep going. Allen, our neighbor, continued the search through the thick of the woods, most of the night. He grew up in these woods and was familiar with the trails.

We all sat around the table in despair, wondering what had taken place at school that these sweet little girls would resort to such a drastic decision. I kept reminding myself to keep the faith, and believe that the Lord would bring them home. We made lots of coffee to keep us alert for the long night ahead.

At 2:00 a.m. my faith began to slip a little. Frightful feelings continued to stir in my mind. I just knew if Wendy and Jackie were around the area, they would be home by now, or someone would have found them. Harvey and Allen had been out looking for hours, while Jackie's mother and I waited anxiously at the house. Most volunteer groups had gone home for the night. The rain continued in a downpour. We sat quietly in prayer while we were waiting. Harvey and Allen finally came in about 4:00 a.m. with no positive news.

The night moved so slowly that it seemed like an eternity. Morning light was beginning to shine through the windows, as the clock struck 6:00 a.m. I was exhausted from worry and lack of sleep. As we sat with heads hung low, the kitchen door slowly opened, and in walked two wet, muddy little girls. Oh, how my heart jumped for joy at seeing them alive and well! They looked like two rug rats with matted hair, soaked clothes and mud up to their knees. Other than being frightened, they had no other bodily harm. We were so overcome with joy that the thought of punishing them was not in the equation. Everyone was joyfully hugging and kissing these two runaways. Wendy told us they had hiked deep into the woods when the rain forced them to take refuge in a big pile of brush. They were so exhausted that they fell asleep there. At the first peak of daylight, they hurried home.

We waited for the girls to tell us why they ran away. They explained that the teacher had frightened them so badly, that the only logical thing they could think of was to run away. The school was extremely apologetic about the bad communication from the teacher. They had become aware of her attitude with other students, and she was immediately fired from her position.

Without hesitation, we immediately moved Wendy back to LCA, where she attended through the ninth grade. We learned not to make hasty, emotional decisions, based on what our children want. We also learned to wait until we have earnestly prayed for God's direction in the lives of our children.

Chapter 9
THE SACRIFICIAL GIFT

My family and I have always loved being out in nature. I enjoy sitting alone and reminiscing about good memories. One afternoon, I headed to a favorite site, down through the field to my huge oak tree. Laying back against the tree with my glass of tea made the retreat perfect. The blue sky enhanced the beauty of the white clouds; I could see pictures in them. It reminded me of the peaceful times we laid out on blankets at my grandparent's house imagining pictures in the clouds. I could hear the birds chirping from the fence as if they were talking to each other.

I was about to doze off when a sweet memory filled my head and heart. A couple of days after we lost Wendy, we were all saddened, yet we were joyful that Wendy was with Jesus. During that time, visitors and family were coming to pay their respects and share their love. Even though the comfort of loved ones is very appreciated, it is very tiring. Most people did not have the words to express their sorrow. Although I hurt deep in my heart and soul, I tried to convince myself not to sink into negative thoughts. Wendy would not want me to go there.

The front doorbell rang, and I wondered who would be coming in that door since we always used the kitchen door. When I saw who it was, I felt tremendous relief as my Grandmother and Aunt Faye came in. For the first time since Wendy's death, I expressed happiness and knew that everything would be all right. Grandma was our family's backbone and spiritual leader and my Aunt Faye had a servant's heart.

Grandma's visit hurt me and lifted me at the same time. She had to muster up all the energy she had to devote time to me. Cancer had worked against her for a long time, and now she was in the last stage of this terrible disease. As we shared a big hug, I clung to her and didn't want to let go. I laid my head on her shoulder and sobbed. Both Grandma and Faye had advanced arthritis for many years. Faye, a strong, God-fearing woman, would not allow Satan to get a foothold with her health. To stay active, she kept pressing on in high gear. Using her cane to walk to a chair, Grandma took a seat by me and placed a beautiful bag beside her chair. Sitting there, I pondered to myself, "What do people do in times like these if they don't know Jesus or have the support of their family and friends?"

When things settled down, Grandma pulled the bag into her lap. Her knotted arthritic fingers and hands looked painful as she opened the bag. "Violet," she said, "Faye and I have been working on something for you, and completed it in record time." All eyes were on Grandma as she pulled out a beautiful, king-size quilt from the bag. "Oohh's & Aahh's!" filled the room when she displayed this masterpiece of patchwork colors. It reminded me of Joseph's coat of many colors. I felt so very special to be loved that much. It was truly a sacrificial gift made from the heart, and one to cherish all of my life. Big crocodile tears dropped off my lids onto the blanket that was draped over our laps. Grandma's quilt stayed close by whenever Tim, Harvey and I wanted to curl up together on the sofa. At other times, I folded it up and placed it at the foot of our bed.

My grandmother died a few months after we buried Wendy. She left priceless mementos behind that we have shared for years. We have read some of her poems and enjoyed the drawings that she created while in college. I can't believe we had never seen them before. She scribbled her daily journal on calendars, and did this, right up to her last days. One particular entry made me sad when she wrote, "It's a rainy Sunday, and I am very lonesome; none of the family came to visit today. I am down in the dumps."

Although Grandma taught us many things, her greatest legacy passed on to me was her influence and discipline as a Christian grandmother. She was a role model for all of us to follow. Each night, after everyone was back in the house, we would all retire to the dining room, which also had a sitting area. Grandma was a Sunday-School teacher, and she would sit at the table with her Bible and her lesson book, pull little Sheilla onto her lap and start reading. Other times she read from family history books. We were always excited when she got to the part about our relative, Samuel Clements (Mark Twain) and his brother, John. The children in the family would sometimes copy this section for a school project. After Grandma was done reading it was prayer time, then early to bed and early to rise at our grandmother and grandfather's house in the country.

Now that Grandma is in heaven with Wendy and my mother, I envision her describing the quilt during their heavenly walks through fields of bright, vibrant flowers nurtured by the light and love of our Almighty Father. We only see a mere fraction of His creation here on Earth. As I sat under the grand old oak tree viewing His creation, I tried to imagine the majestic splendor of heaven. Taking these time-outs from our busy lives sends good health through our bodies and calms our spirits. As the Bible says, "Be still and know…"

Chapter 10
MOTHER BURIED HER UNHEALED WOUNDS

Today is my mother's birthday; oh, how I miss her so very much. There are so many memories of her that are dear to my heart. Her sacrifice for us children had come from supernatural strength.

Deep in the heart of my mother resided past wounds that she buried into her subconscious mind. For many years, she suffered physical and emotional abuse from my alcoholic father, who also caused angst-ridden stress in my brother and me. My younger sisters were too young to remember witnessing my father physically and mentally tormenting my mother. Over the years, those memories left me with a disheartened anxiety; not to mention what it did to her. My mom was a fragile woman who drew on her inner-strength from God. Her courage was undeniable as she grabbed up her little children and left.

For years, when horrible memories of my early childhood flooded my mind, I would brood over the pain and hardship my mother had to endure. I don't like to admit it, but I carried hate for my father. Then, seven years ago, freedom rang out loud and clear, bringing peace to my heart and soul. With the help of a good friend and caregiver, I reached deep down inside and released my many hurts, fears, and anxieties to the Lord Jesus. After placing them at His feet, those painful burdens lifted, and a new mindset transformed my thinking.

WHY?

After my mother left my father, she became the leader and sustainer in our lives. We depended on her for soothing our hurts, giving support, providing for our needs, and loving us unconditionally. Enriching our spiritual life, and moral values, were first and foremost to my mother. Being a single mother at that time was extremely difficult, and people gave her credit for raising such fine children. She didn't send us to church; she led us to church. She also encouraged us to participate in activities. Always leading by example, she became a teacher of a girl's class, and she sang in the choir.

Sacrificing her comforts for her children was relevant to who my mother was. She denied herself the personal comforts of life to provide for us. Out of necessity, she had to work outside of the home. She took leftover beans on sandwiches for her lunch and gave us the meat and cheese, which had to last all week. Not understanding her sacrifice, out of love, we took it for granted. I wonder if sometimes we do the same thing with Jesus.

Rain, sleet, or snow, my mother walked six blocks to catch a bus for work, and she never missed a day. It was so hard to make ends meet, but my proud mother finally accepted my grandfather's help with the expenses. He worked a full-time job and owned a small business on the side. Because of that, he was able to help my mother.

My mom not only worked hard to keep our family together, but she also worked hard at making us feel special. She encouraged us by reminding us that we were smart, of good character and integrity. I began to believe her encouraging statement, "You children can do anything you set your minds to do. It doesn't matter what you have; it's who you are."

I'll never forget her influence on me when I was in fifth grade. My teacher loved music and spent time each week teaching the class to sing and play musical instruments. One afternoon she asked those who had instruments to bring them in on Friday. The only instrument I played was an upright piano my grandmother had given me. I asked my mom, "What

10: *Mother Buried Her Unhealed Wounds*

can I do? I can't take the piano to school." In her can-do spirit, she tore off a piece of wax paper, wrapped it around a comb and taught me to use my voice to hum a song through it. I questioned the reality of this comb being an instrument. My mother described it as a "unique instrument." She made it such a big deal that I felt more willing to take it to school.

That Friday, the teacher called up each instrument, one at a time. Clarinets, flutes, and trumpets rang out all over the room and down the hall. Then it was my turn to perform. All the kids stared awkwardly when I eagerly marched to the front of the classroom with a comb in my hand. My mom had taught me a lively tune, and I toe-tapped at the same time as I played. I noticed some of my friends tapping also. Amazingly, my teacher was so impressed with the uniqueness of my instrument, and my effort, that she selected me to go around to the other classes and perform.

My mother also encouraged my sister, Jan, when she was in kindergarten. She was assigned "Frosty the Snowman" to sing at the Christmas program in front of students and parents. If you knew Jan as we did, you would know that it took much encouraging, or maybe even a miracle, but my mom was persistent. On the other hand, my feisty sister, Sheilla would stand up and try anything. "Oh, I can do that." She would say with confidence, and she did it.

Sheilla was the youngest, and she had a lot of spunk. She was determined never to cry when my mother had to switch her. In those days, we had to retrieve our switches. Once we watched Sheilla go around and around while our mother tried to hold her and switch her at the same time. Two determined spirits were at war. Thinking back, I believe mother tired out before Sheilla. Jan, on the other hand, stayed on the skirt-tails of mother and became her little helper.

All of us girls paired up and outnumbered our brother, Preston, who had a room to himself, which he declared off-limits to silly girls. He took care of all his belongings and kept them neatly placed. He needed a male figure to help guide and encourage him, so our Uncles' Monnie and Wray rallied around for him at times.

Although we all had separate interests, we shared in family activities. It made my mom happy when we all gathered around the old piano and sang hymns. Even though my piano skills needed some work, thankfully, no one knew enough to criticize. Jan liked to request her favorite hymn, "Standing on the Promises." We never had a sing-along without including the song, "In the Garden." Every once in a while, just for fun, I would sneak in a little Boogie-woogie. My mother would jump in there and dance the "Charleston."

We were always excited for Friday night. It was hamburgers and French fries night at home. It seems like such a little thing now, but there were times mother would take a break from cooking, and she would have us meet her at the Avenue café called the Tiny Tavern. It was a tiny place, but it was nice to have someone else cook our burgers for a change. On Saturday nights, we all sat around with a bowl of popcorn and watched 'The Grand Ole Opry' on television.

Christmas time was exciting around our house. We each received two presents and clothes, which we did not consider a Christmas gift. We had no stockings hanging by the chimney, just shoeboxes on the mantel, filled with all kinds of fruit, nuts, and candy. That tradition always put us in a happy mood. My mother would lay out our old torn book, with the story of Christmas. To me, it was mainly the spirit of Christmas and special events that brought joy and happiness. Things like going to church plays, singing Christmas carols door to door, visits from Aunt Faye and her family, and neighbors dropping in at our house.

When Preston and I were little kids, we spent many summers in the country with Grandma and Granddad Coleman. Usually, after a big dinner, the adults sat on the front porch with ice tea and the newspaper, while we played in the yard. We didn't retreat inside until dusk when we would hear

10: *Mother Buried Her Unhealed Wounds*

Violet & Preston, who went to heaven early

the whip-poor-wills chanting his name.

Taking a break from my mother did not give us permission to dodge going to church. Our grandmother would never hear of such a thing. We learned many Bible verses and made crafts in Vacation Bible School. On the eve of the last day, parents would gather to watch the students perform. Preston and I had a favorite song, and we went around singing it all the time. Grandma promised us a toy of our choice if we would sing in front of the whole church. It wasn't until we were encouraged by my mother that we reluctantly agreed. Grandma didn't forget; I got my jump rope and Preston got a train set. I'm not too sure that was really fair.

When we were older, we took care of ourselves in the summer. My mother would leave each of us twenty-five cents, which paid for swimming at Riverside pool, and enough left over for snacks to munch on all the way home. We got our exercise walking the Avenue each day. And, oh yes, there was the anticipated excitement of the twice a summer, Saturday night dance at our local elementary school on the tennis court. The tennis nets were taken down. Chairs lined the court, and a small stage was set up

WHY GOD WHY?

for the band. These were times when we didn't jump in the car to drive everywhere, we walked. Of course, all young folks had to be accompanied by their parents. We all had so much fun as we laughed, talked and danced throughout the evening. Back then girls could dance together without people calling them names.

About seven years after mother's divorce, she started seeing a nice looking fellow who was about to graduate from Lynchburg College. He was an older student returning for a master's degree. As they grew closer and fell very much in love, my mother worried about what it would do to her children if she were to remarry. We were not very receptive to their relationship. Once again, mother exhibited her sacrificial love for us by breaking off the relationship. We could tell that she was hurt and lonesome, but as usual, she always put her children first.

In time, all us children married and started our families. We all made frequent visits to my mother's house and enjoyed her delicious meals. She lived to make us happy and comfortable. My mom always shared her recipes with us girls, along with a little love note. She journaled every single day, as did her mother, so we have many of her precious words to remember her by and keep in our hearts.

Before she died, my mother requested the song, "I'll Rise Again," which was Wendy's favorite song, to be sung at her funeral. My mother is not with us now; she is in heaven with Wendy, Grandma, and all the other loved ones that went on before her. I imagine they stood at the heavenly gates waiting to greet my mom when she arrived.

After my mother had died, Jan, Sheilla, and I, each took a box filled with books and pictures. A few weeks later, we discovered that each of us had a Bible that had belonged to our mother. Tucked throughout the pages of all three Bibles were her poems, drawings and other cherished clippings of her children's accomplishments. Another thing I found was a letter from my son, Tim, written to his grandma from college, which reflected his love for her and appreciation for her spiritual leadership. She wrote to him and kept up with him while he was away. As we continued to look through her Bibles, we found that my mom earmarked many of her favorite Bible verses. Mother always clung to her favorite verse, *"I can do all things through Christ, who strengthens me."*

Preston went to be with Jesus a few years ago, at an early age. Jan and Sheilla, my two sisters and I get together every Wednesday to visit and chat. We call it our therapy day. Occasionally, we talk about our mother and the strength she must have had. Even though her life was not easy, she never lost faith. She left a legacy of that faith for each one of us to emulate.

Chapter 11
WHY FIVE YEARS TO THE DAY, LORD?

With all the battering of Tim's little body, it gave us reason to wonder if he would make it to fatherhood. At the age of two, he had some small toy accidents, but as he got older, they turned into tough-boy mishaps. Imagine a two-year-old almost killing himself on a toy chicken! Not once, but twice did that crazy chicken cause Tim to be knocked unconscious at the same place. Tim would rear back on that thing like he was riding a horse, flip over backward, and hit his head on the concrete patio.

A few years later, there was that darn tree that kept stepping out in front of his bicycle; then it was the dirt bike accident sending him to the hospital. And then it was that nest of bees he hit with the lawnmower. Who would have known he was allergic to bees? I could put up with the chicken, the tree, and even the bees, but not that big yellow Lincoln that hit Tim as he crossed the highway on his bike. He had been on his way to ball practice at the local field.

For five years, that particular day had brought gloom to my heart and soul. It was five years to-the-day that Wendy and Tim were in that horrible accident in which we lost Wendy. I knew God had a purpose for Wendy and was beginning to accept His plan for her life and death. My faith grew along the way. I had learned to appreciate October 5th and

WHY GOD WHY?

busied myself as Director of Information Systems at work. Although the accident still crossed my mind, I was too busy to linger in those thoughts. Jobs were flowing in, computers and printers churning away, and programmers deep into applications. It was a very intense day with unusual demands and schedules to meet.

Just when I thought I had all I could stand this day, an emergency phone call put me to the test. It was Déjà vu. That day—exactly five years after the accident—was about to emulate the horrible day that had altered our lives forever. My secretary informed me that I had a phone call waiting, and it sounded urgent. I didn't recognize the shaky voice on the other end. I finally realized it was my next door neighbor. She said, "Violet, it's Marjorie! A young man ran from the highway to my door when he found you were not at home. He was screaming that Tim had been hit by a car and is lying in a ditch and not moving!"

I lost control of myself and panicked as I threw the phone and ran down the hall screaming and crying, "Tim has been hit by a car and is lying in a ditch!" Carol Johnson, my senior programmer, offered to drive me to the accident scene. My sister Sheilla, who was also employed there, was telephoning Harvey to inform him.

We couldn't travel fast enough for me. My voice was shaky as I prayed desperately to the Lord, just as I had after Wendy's accident. The clock began to turn back with memories of that October 5, 1980, accident with Wendy and Tim. Trying to console my emotions, I mentally repeated God's Word and His promises. However, the 'Why's' kept filling my mind. Why God? Why these horrible accidents with our children? And why five years to the day? I received no immediate answers, and my fear did not subside. Keeping strong faith in times like these is very hard, but I knew that was what I needed to do.

We were about three miles from the accident scene when a rescue truck with sirens blaring flashed by us going in the opposite direction toward the

11: Why Five Years to the Day, Lord?

hospital. I just knew Tim was in that truck. Carol pulled into a nearby business where I phoned and got confirmation that Tim was on his way to the hospital. We broke all speeding records trying to catch the rescue squad. I didn't know how badly he was hurt, or if he was even alive.

Carol pulled up to the hospital emergency area to let me out. I frantically ran to the information desk asking for my Tim. Telling me to take a seat was not acceptable. Yelling to see my son brought immediate attention, and I was escorted to the bay area. Rescue workers were standing around this gurney, and I knew it had to be Tim. I was never so happy to see him. He was sitting there talking with the staff. Thankfully, his injuries were not life-threatening. The calf on the back of his leg was torn very badly and crushed deeply into his leg. His body was decorated with bruises and scratches from head to toe. The doctor said he was one lucky young boy. He ordered Tim to use a wheelchair for two weeks, then crutches for support. Tim exited the hospital in a wheelchair and with bandages.

Harvey and I were informed about the details surrounding the accident. Tim was heading to ball practice on his bicycle when a lady in a speeding Lincoln hit him dead center as he was crossing the highway. Witnesses said the impact knocked Tim about six feet into the air. On his descent, the car hit him again, knocking him into a ditch where she swerved and nearly ran him over. Tim laid unconscious while others tried to console and care for him.

It was like history repeating itself, Tim's present teacher, Mrs. Joyce Zug, happened to be driving by and offered Tim comfort. Tim was very fond of Mrs. Zug, and she loved Tim. Another 'Why God?' flashed through my thoughts. Was it a coincidence that both of Tim's teachers were present at his near-death accidents? And, was it a coincidence that the two accidents were five years apart, to the day?

It took a while, but Tim's leg finally began to heal, and the bruises faded. A large indented scar became a permanent reminder of the acci-

WHY GOD WHY?

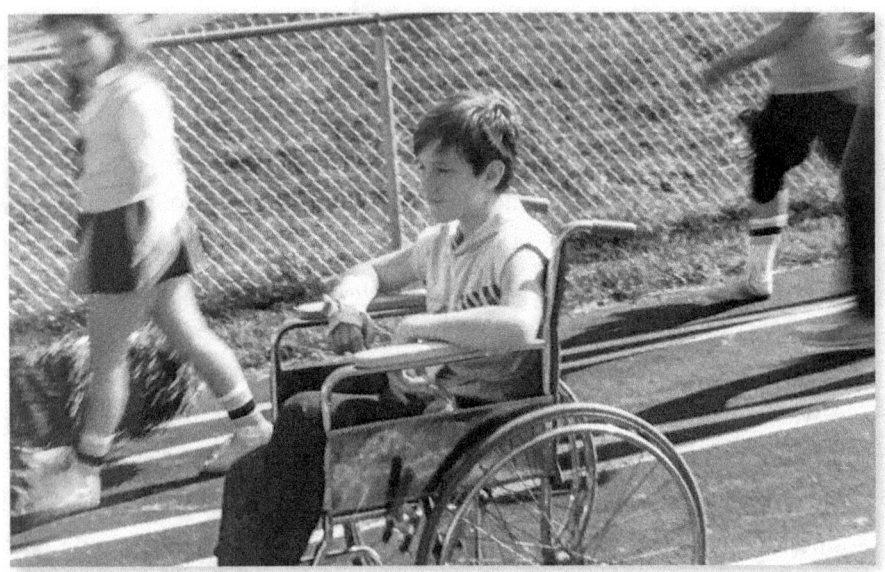

Tim cheered his team on from the sidelines

dent. He was unable to participate playing in the games because of his injuries, but he was able to watch his championship game in his wheelchair, from the sidelines. He wanted to get out on that field so very badly. He followed each of the plays of the game, up and down the track, steering that wheelchair.

Harvey and I both knew that the doctor was wrong. It was not luck that saved Tim's life; it was divine intervention from God. I don't know the answers to my 'why' questions. I do know that God has a purpose for the things that happen in our lives. We could ask 'why' and moan forever about our son's accidents, or we could thank the Lord and give Him the glory for sparing Tim's life and for later giving us three awesome grandchildren.

Chapter 12
AN UPSIDE DAY WITH A DOWNSIDE ENDING

We have had some shadows in our lives, but we have also had many wonderful times, especially with our longtime friends, Deda and Johnny. We have shared many years together, the good times and the bad. Thankfully it's been mostly good times that have given us years of joy and laughter, including this day.

It was one of many pleasant days boating on Smith Mountain Lake right up to the last hour. Mid-morning, Deda, Johnny, Harvey and I jumped on the pontoon boat for a wonderful day on the lake. While boarding, an enormous snake slithered from the rocks into the water beside us, and my skin crawled with chills. I kept thinking of that poisonous viper throughout the day. This made-to-order day soon helped me forget about that horrible creature. The breeze was blowing in our hair as we slowly cruised along the coastline drinking soda pop and snacking on chips. Deda and I were lounging in the sun, and as usual, we chattered intensely. We both have the gift of gab, while simultaneously using our radar to pick up on Harvey and Johnny's conversation. Men claim they don't talk as much as women, but I would place my money against that claim.

We always got around to reminiscing about old times and things that made us laugh. Once we were at a function, and we both had to visit the

WHY GOD WHY?

restroom. I couldn't find the flusher. Therefore, I was pushing screws on the wall and anything else that might flush the thing. I began to laugh and so did Deda, as she confessed, "Can you find the flusher?" "No," I said. People outside the stall doors were laughing. Then I noticed that the seat pointed at a slight angle toward the ceiling. I put my foot on top of it and pushed down. Voila! The commode flushed. That's when I figured out the problem; if you don't sit on these restroom seats, they will not flush.

As we neared the lake home of Deda's sister, we decided to dock the boat and take a swim. We floated around in the refreshing water and talked for a couple more hours before dressing for dinner. The boathouse was locked, so the only place to change clothes was on the steps leading to the top deck. While holding up my towel and stepping into my pants, I grabbed the side of the building for support. My hand slid down and caught a large splinter in my palm. Harvey tugged at that splinter until it finally released, but it left my hand sore to the touch.

All decked out for dinner; we motored back to the dock to return the boat. People were standing around watching Harvey steer into the same docking slip from the morning. I jumped up on the front ledge of the boat making sure we cleared the poles. Just as I reached out for the pole, Harvey accidentally clipped the back end of the dock bringing the boat to an abrupt halt. The jolt threw me into a complete somersault and into the water leaving a great splash visible. You've heard the phrase, "Man overboard!" With little space between the boat and the rocks, I struggled to the surface; however, my feet, with my brand new sandals, were stuck about ten inches into the oozy mud. Suddenly, I remembered that this is where I had seen that snake. I went into panic mode, kicking for dear life and had to sacrifice one of my new sandals to the thick mud. I finally surfaced, screaming like a wild person. My darling husband and my wonderful friends were laughing themselves silly.

12: *An Upside Day with a Downside Ending*

After safely boarding the boat again, all three of those scallywags began laughing at my appearance and this bizarre incident. I didn't think it was funny as I sat in my soaking wet dinner clothes with only one shoe. "But Violet, Johnny said, you did such a perfect somersault, it was as if you staged it." Of course, I was embarrassed as the onlookers saw my appearance. There were more chuckles from the pier, as I struggled to get in the back seat of the car to change back into my wet swimsuit.

Finally, I got back into the boat to gather our belongings and help load them into the car. Since we had rocks to walk through, I slipped on Harvey's size eleven sandals. The boat was about twelve inches below the dock level, and my arms were full as I proceeded to step up. The unusual chain of events continued for the day. The toe of that oversized sandal caught under the dock and down I went like a plump chicken throwing everything everywhere. In the process, I broke my thumb sending severe pain through my hand and up my arm. In agony, I looked up for sympathy. They did not know I had broken my thumb; they began to chuckle with laughter again. It must have been hilarious to watch. Deda found a cup and filled it with ice for my thumb as it began to swell, and the pain grew more severe. She drove me forty minutes to a medical center back in town, while Johnny and Harvey followed on their motorcycles.

Holding my thumb in that cup, I entered the medical center wearing Harvey's sandals, a wet swimsuit, and a short tee shirt. I was a sight to behold. With bulging eyes, the desk clerk looked me over while taking my insurance information. Standing in a room full of curious people was so embarrassing. Not to mention, I am no light-weight.

There was a pretty long wait before they finally called my name to be seen by, none other than ... "Oh No!" I said to Deda, "Tom is the physician on call tonight." He is my longtime doctor and friend. Deda accompanied me into the examining room where the nurse gave me a stool to climb onto a table for observation. In a short while, Dr. Tom

WHY GOD WHY?

entered the room with a little grin on his face. These types of memories, whether they are embarrassing or funny, are the ones we remember years later and cherish.

As he examined my thumb, I began to fill his ears with my lake story. Right at the funny part of the story, Tom had to leave the room. The nurse took an x-ray of my thumb showing that it indeed was broken. I finished telling Tom my story, and Deda laughed all over again as if it just happened.

Doctor Tom explained that my thumb needed to be set, and we needed to move to another room. As he helped me off the table, the long paper stuck to my wet swimsuit and followed me to the door. When Tom pulled the paper off, a large imprint of my bottom was perfectly displayed on the paper. Awkwardly embarrassed, I wondered if this day was a curse from hell.

Harvey and Johnny joined us for the procedure. Tom asked me to brace myself, as he inflicted pain with a big jerk of my thumb. A loud popping noise pierced the room, followed by Harvey and Johnny verbally moaning. Tom insisted they leave the room if they could not take the heat, as he chuckled under his breath. Well, they did just that, while Deda stayed behind with me. Dr. Tom finally displayed humor over the lake incident.

Over the years, the four of us shared many laughs over that day at the lake. Oh yes, I also laugh with them. These types of memories whether they are embarrassing or funny are the ones we remember years later and wind up cherishing more than anything else. I thank God for these wonderful friends and the memories that have filled our lives with laughter.

Chapter 13
UNFORGIVING TRIP TO DENVER

Either Harvey or I needed to attend a software show in Denver with the intention of purchasing software for Harvey's business venture. Although I don't like to fly, drawing the short straw put me in the position to represent his company at a software presentation in Denver, Colorado. A friend who is also a colleague made all the arrangements including the session, flight and accommodation bookings. The itinerary listed my flying into Denver where I would catch a commuter flight to 'No-Man's Land,' Colorado. I say that because no one had ever heard of the town.

The flight to Denver was smooth and uneventful, but I wasn't sure where to board the commuter flight. An unfriendly airport employee pointed me down a long corridor, to the down steps. I followed the signs to the outside flight patio, where I saw this thing that looked like a toy airplane. "Do you mean to tell me this two-seater is my commuter flight?" I asked the service attendant outside.

Out of nowhere appeared this young fellow with a fearless attitude wearing a baseball cap. "This is going to be a story to write home about," I imagined, as he introduced himself as Mike, my private pilot for the day. Before takeoff, the young pilot announced, "Buckle up and rest back; we're going to have an adventurous trip." I knew this guy was a show-off, and I was not ready for an adventure.

WHY GOD WHY?

The takeoff felt like one of those, suck you under, butterfly rides at amusement parks. After two minutes in the air, this smart-aleck informed me that he was going to dip the plane down and show me some interesting sights on the way. I was about to ask what 'dip down' meant, but it was too late.

I thought I would have a heart attack when he turned the nose straight to the ground and leveled out over a baseball game at the stadium. I felt as if we were in a military bombing aircraft. Suddenly, it began to rain very hard, and I could not see out the window very well. "How can he see if I can't?" I asked myself. The wind picked up and the 'Little Plane That Could' started to shake, rattle and roll.

The rain had cleared when the pilot finally pointed out the destination airport coming up. There was only one landing strip and a small metal building for a terminal. As we came around for our landing approach, another aircraft was coming around from another direction and heading directly for us. Suddenly, the force of our steep climb to avoid a collision pushed me against the back of my seat like a suction tube. My pilot was yelling angrily at the other pilot's wrong approach. I was so relieved when we finally landed that toy. The pilot taxied over to a small building no larger than my kitchen and escorted me out of the plane. "Is this where I am supposed to be?" I asked. Here I was in the middle of nowhere with no one waiting for me.

I asked the farmers inside if I could use the phone to call my colleague. They pointed to a phone booth outside the building. Once I finally got connected, I could not believe what I heard on the other end. My colleague apologized profusely, admitting she had wrongly sent me to the town of the software developers, who are conducting the show. Good grief, I wanted to scream! The show is in Denver where I landed in the first place—75 miles away.

John, one of the owners, had agreed to come for me at the airport. Getting in the car with a complete stranger was very uncomfortable for

13: *Unforgiving Trip to Denver*

me. However, the way my day had gone so far, this was no shock. John introduced himself and told me how busy he was putting the packages together for the show in Denver. He asked if I would mind going with him back to the office and help him make copies of the package inserts. Afterward, he would try to find me a motel room somewhere nearby. "God," I silently prayed, "I don't know where this is going, however, You are in charge."

After a couple hours of copying and inserting, John called for motel information. We drove across town to a section that was a little scary to me. Pulling up into this place called Dream Land Motel made me think of a horror movie I had seen. John said his goodbyes and told me he would pick me up in the morning.

I had not eaten all day, and my stomach was a little upset, and I was exhausted. Looking around, I did see a small take-out pizza shop across the street. At least I wouldn't starve to death. Retiring for the night, I thought about all of the other participants sleeping in luxury at the Denver Convention Center hotel.

Not knowing what time they were coming for me, I got up at the crack of dawn, and was ready when they arrived. As they drove up to my door, I thought, "Oh, no, I am still in this nightmare." The two owners of the software company and one other fellow arrived in a pickup truck with a closed body on the back. One of the three men gave up his seat for me in the cab and climbed in the back with all the computers. Here I was, stuffed in the truck between these two fellows I didn't know, and I was very uncomfortable. It was inconceivable to me that these guys were putting on a huge, nationally advertised software show.

The Denver Hotel was a happy sight to see. The hotel was clean and plush, therefore, I had no need of looking under the bed for bedbugs. Later, I ran into my escorts, and they acted as if they had never seen me before. Right then, I knew I wasn't getting a discount on my software purchase.

The presentation was very informative, and the package was just what we needed for our business.

My return trip back home was quiet and relaxing, and it gave me plenty of time to think about this crazy adventure. Deda, Johnny, and Harvey were not surprised about this unbelievable story of my trip to Denver. Deda only suggested, "You need to write a book, Violet."

Chapter 14
FROM HOLY GROUND TO HOLY TERROR

The dream of going to Israel had been on the forefront of my mind from an early age. I always thought—"I'll never get there." Fortunately, the front was not influenced by the back. Harvey always says, "Never say never."

In 1985, while employed by Dr. Jerry Falwell's ministries, my dream came true. I was ecstatic when they asked if I would like to travel with the team to Israel and participate as an event leader and table host. This employee benefit was far beyond my greatest expectation. To add sugar to my cup, Harvey and Tim had the privilege of traveling with me. "Lord, what have I done to deserve this dream-come-true trip?"

Preparing for our first trip out of the country made me a bit anxious. The thought of flying over water for twelve hours gave me goose bumps. I had never traveled out of the United States. The first leg of the trip, from Lynchburg to New York's Kennedy Airport, was a cinch. Checking through to another country was much more detailed and tiresome than we had imagined. Still excited, we boarded this huge aircraft that had an upper cabin, four large movie screens, about fifty lavatories and more seats than I could see. "How in the world can this airplane lift off the ground with the weight of all the luggage and hundreds of passengers?" I questioned Harvey.

WHY GOD
WHY?

We were assigned first-class seats, on the main level. Usually first class is behind the pilot's cabin and attendant's station. Oddly, we were directly in the nose of the plane. My next thought was, "If this thing spirals to the ground, we will be human butter." The pilots and other first-class passengers were on the next level connected by spiral steps. I stayed glued to my seat most of the trip. My legs were numb, and my back was tired. I was hoping to see water; however, these flights are almost always at night. Tim, Harvey, and other people were roaming the cabins, but not me. I was even too nervous to get up to use the restroom.

Checking out of Kennedy Airport seemed strict, but the scrutiny with customs in Tel Aviv was very tense, to say the least. After lengthy checkpoints, we quickly boarded the tour buses assigned to our large group. Each bus had an Israeli tour guide. However, as one of the staff assistants, I made sure each person assigned to our bus was accounted for after each event or site trip.

Relaxing in the first hotel was nice, but the food was foremost on our minds as we moved into the main dining room for dinner. Hungry or not, looking at a fish looking back at me was not my cup of tea. A sweet Trinidad lady who was at our table, latched on to Tim and became his shadow throughout the trip.

We toured many religious sites, many of which we remembered from Biblical studies. One of the places we stopped was the Dome of the Rock—this is considered sacred ground. It is thought to be the place where Abraham attempted to sacrifice Isaac. The beauty inside the Dome was awesome. We exited out the side door down to a very sacred platform with a small flow of water around it. Not having our guide with us, we were not aware of the sacredness of this site. We were to find out that this is where the male Jews take off their shoes and wash their feet before moving onto the platform to kneel and pray. We turned our backs for just a moment; lo and behold, Tim was on top of that sacred platform, and with his shoes on

14: *From Holy Ground to Holy Terror*

his feet. Before we could get to him, an old Jewish man grabbed him by the neck with his cane, pulled him down and set him on a wall. I didn't know the nature of these people and was afraid that he might hurt Tim. He began to loudly scold Tim explaining the sacred importance of that praying fountain. Tim was stunned at first, but then the man became calmer as he took the Jewish headdress that we purchased as a souvenir for Tim, removed it from Tim's head, and wrapped it back correctly. He showed kindness and talked with Tim a while longer before our departure.

Next, off to the Wailing Wall in Jerusalem where the Jewish people pray intensely. Beyond this area were many alleyways filled with historical artifacts and many

Tim learned how to wrap the headdress the hard way

merchant tents. After we viewed the model of Jerusalem and listened to the guide talk about some of the history, we were free to tour the city which was surrounded by a large rock wall. I found myself wandering through the dim alleyways where merchants were enticing me. Suddenly, I realized I was alone. Where was Harvey, Tim, and the others? Here I was, lost in the middle of these dark alleys of merchant tents with fear plastered on my face. These people were strange to me, and I was afraid. Not knowing which way to run, I just started running as fast as I could. As

WHY GOD WHY?

I exited the other end of this maze, I was so happy to see familiar faces. Harvey and Tim had worried about me, but all was well. After getting to know the sincerity of the Jewish people, I felt secure enough to shop alone the very next day.

We ate fish at the Sea of Galilee, just like the disciples. That fish was delicious. Checking into a hotel, we relaxed before our next venture. Some of the ladies asked if Tim could go with them to the Bethlehem Baptist Church. I was leery about allowing him to go because the area where we had stayed the previous night was bombed by enemies of Israel. Harvey finally gave Tim permission to go, and they left in a taxi. On their way to the church, rebels stormed the taxi and began to throw stones at them. Fearful for his life, the driver dumped Tim and the ladies out in the middle of the street. Although they were frightened, they continued on the journey to Bethlehem. We caught up with them later and watched a film of the crucifixion.

The next day, we toured some of the cities up high in the mountains. People lived in small places built on the side of the mountain. It was scary driving on such small roads. Returning down was a task since the driver had no sizeable place to turn around. He turned in the middle of the road and backed up until the back of the bus was hanging over a very high cliff. I ran to the front yelling, "STOP! We are going over!" He kept backing up, and I kept yelling as I feared for my life. My heart was about to jump out of my chest. When he finally stopped, I was a basket case. Then I sat down by Harvey and held his hand. I could not believe he was laughing at me for getting so excited. That's a man for you.

Traveling by the Dead Sea, we saw many natural, hot springs shooting straight up into the air. Of course, Tim had to test the mysterious Dead Sea which contains so many minerals that you can't sink. Without moving his arms, Tim just lay there on the water as if he were on a float. He loved having the chance to try everything.

14: *From Holy Ground to Holy Terror*

We saw the mountain called Masada. Tim and Harvey entered the cable car and waved to me as they ascended the mountain, because I was too scared to travel to the top. Tile floors were still visible with colors of beauty. This was where the Jewish people took refuge from the Roman army. It was unbelievable that they protected themselves for such a long time before the soldiers finally reached them; however, they did not have a defeat. The Jewish people took poison to die in a less tortured fashion. The stories of what Harvey and Tim saw and learned was awesome.

The two most heartfelt places were Golgotha and the tomb of Christ our Lord. Being inside His tomb visualizing the scene was undoubtedly an experience I will never forget. The stone door lay back exposing the curvature opening that we entered. Standing where Jesus stood, in the shadows of the tomb, was an out-of-body experience. It was eerie. The feeling was powerful. I could almost hear, "He has risen, He is not here!" Humbleness filled my heart and soul as I thought about the Lord dying on the cross for my sins, and rising from the grave that third day, as He said He would.

We were part of the group who were also going to tour Egypt. Our entrance into Egyptian customs made the Tel Aviv airport look timid. Egyptians do not like Israelis, and since our plane came from Israel, they were hard and abrupt. They cut the whole front of my suitcase open to check inside, then they taped it up with duct tape and nearly threw it to me.

Pharaoh's tomb and the pyramids appeared just as I had seen them in books. Tim ran ahead of everyone, and it was hard to keep him in our sight. He got to experience camel riding, and he certainly enjoyed showing off his stuff.

In the city of Cairo, we passed many men with several wives following them. We witnessed a funeral procession as they carried their dead walking down the middle of the street. Small cars were running in and out of traffic at high rates of speed. We experienced a boat trip down the Nile that was unbelievable. People lived in mud huts where animals were running

WHY GOD WHY?

Between Israel and Egypt, Tim became a pro on camel

in and out. If you looked close enough, you could see beautiful children underneath mud-covered faces.

The day we were to depart and head back home, the tour guide told us to eat in the dining hall where they had the food prepared for us. He had warned us not to eat beef in the hotel restaurant. What did Tim and Harvey do? Those two stubborn guys went down into the restaurant and ordered hamburgers. I have no idea where Tim and Harvey were when they made the warning announcements, but I'm here to tell you, they paid for it all the way back on the flight to the United States.

Many times we have looked at the pictures and slides from that memorable trip. We were blessed to walk where our Lord walked, and to see the places where He was crucified and buried. Our Savior brought victory over the grave for all. I will forever hold the memories of that trip in my heart.

Chapter 15
HE GAVE US THE GREEN LIGHT; WE GAVE HIM THE GLORY

For quite some time, Harvey had talked about us starting a business together. He had already thought it through and was very positive about the idea. "Honey, your background in the technical field and my background in business would complement each other. Information management and related services would be right in your comfort zone," he articulated. I was not as enthusiastic about his vision and was not sure if this was a direction God wanted for us. We had experienced, personal and business hurts along the way, therefore, my insecurity left me unsure if this was the right decision.

During our first little business adventure, a friend had convinced Harvey that rental property investment was the way to go. We invested our little savings into renovating and furnishing a house in the old section of the city.

The first renter was a lady with two children. Thirty days later, while collecting the rent, we found out that her family had grown from three to twelve. The second month, they could not pay the rent, so we extended the due date two weeks. When we returned to collect the rent we found they had all moved out, taking everything that wasn't nailed down. No, I have to take that back. They not only stole the furniture, but they also cut away the linoleum rugs in the kitchen and dining room right up to the molding. Unimaginably, they cut the steps off the back porch and burned them in the fireplace for heat, leaving no exit to the back yard. Even though we had installed a new oil heater in the house, they didn't want to purchase oil to heat the house.

Here we were, back to square one, and in such a short time. The walls needed painting again, the furniture was gone, and the plank fence that Harvey had spent so much time on was knocked down. Did we learn anything from this first investment venture? Yes, Harvey had grown and learned many things from the family building business. He had learned a lot from his dad about building, but that was not satisfying for Harvey Hamilton.

In 1985, Harvey had a vision to start a business that would involve me. It would require a lot of responsibility and dedication. We meditated and chatted a long while before we settled on an agreement. We spent considerable time seeking the Lord's approval on this new business idea, and we were not implementing anything until we could see a clear, green light from Him.

We learned that God's timing and our timing were not the same. We took long walks, and we prayed most every night for eight months. We audibly spoke from our hearts, "Lord, if you approve of our desire to open this business, we will always give you the glory. And Lord, we will not move on anything until You send us a green light with clarity."

One night, after many months of walking and praying, we witnessed a comet with a long tail shooting across the open sky. I was sure it was a sign for us to pursue our vision. However, we both knew that it was too easy to make that assumption and didn't feel it was a clear green light from the Lord. A close Christian friend suggested that by faith, we step out of the prayer box and watch the Lord lead. God is not going to pull you out of your prayer box. With all that prayer and all the faith, step out.

15: *He Gave Us the Green Light; We Gave Him the Glory*

Things started to happen that opened up paths in a positive direction. The department, where I was working, ceased operation and it was the ideal time to consider our venture. Harvey received funds from a couple of sales that he worked on for a year. Even though we felt like these were signs for us to move forward, it still was not clear enough. Finally, one evening, both Harvey and I, simultaneously, received the green light. Just as he was coming upstairs to inform me that he felt it was time, I was eagerly headed downstairs to tell him the same thing. That was one of the few times we waited on God, and amazingly He gave us the answer at the same time.

We were aware that this would be a costly venture, and we knew that a bank loan would be necessary. A banker friend felt that it was just not a bankable package. We were both so confident about our venture that his opinion did not scare us off. We made changes to our presentation package, went downtown to the largest bank, and met with the Executive Vice-President. We were confident and excited as we presented our package and strategy. Knowing that God was in control, we were ready to accept the outcome, one way or another. The banker got so caught up in our excitement and confidence in our plan that he gave us the loan and welcomed us as a preferred business client.

A friend and entrepreneur had agreed to invest in Valtim; however, late in the game, he had unforeseen issues and had to decline his previous offer. We hired an investment broker who thought we just fell off a turnip truck. He told us he had an investor who wanted 51% of the stock and all checks would be approved by him. We knew that he, himself, was the unscrupulous investor. When this crazy broker tried to sue us for a service fee, the judge threw the book at him.

We rented a 1,500 square foot suite on the lower level of a business complex. We invited many professional people in business, plus friends and family to the open house for Valtim.

WHY GOD WHY?

We informed our staff that our business was from God, and He would get the glory for it all. Our plan was that the Lord was in the driver's seat. Someone mentioned that it was good to be working for a Christian company. "No, we are not a Christian company," I interjected, "we are a company that is owned by Christians." God blessed us from the get-go.

Our first client, a national fundraiser, whom we believed in, and were familiar with, got us off the ground. The word got out to other national fundraisers, and our business began to grow, one client at a time. A couple of marketing firms, which I had worked with before, referred us to their clientele, and on and on we grew.

It was not long before we began to offer other services and had to expand into the suite next door. Within weeks, we bought land, built a new facility, purchased additional equipment, and added many to our staff. Our objective was, and is, to always give excellent service to our clients. After all, this was a God thing, and He would expect excellence.

Valtim became a full-service vendor providing all the necessary applications and services, including warehousing. That new facility has been added to four times. In spite of the drop in the economy, and forced regulations, we have continued to be fruitful. The business facilities grew over the years, from that first 1,500 square feet to 150,000 square feet.

It hasn't all been easy. We have had some definite setbacks along the way. We learned that God's way is always the best way, and we can feel secure in the outcome with God's direction.

Chapter 16
ANGELS PLAYING IN THE CLOUDS

I contemplated long and hard before deciding to put this down in black and white. People believe in the usual things seen through their eyes and have a narrow spectrum of God's divine power. I'm not the kind of person who sees visions or has had any out-of-the-ordinary premonitions. It's not that I don't believe people have seen unusual things if God so wishes. Nevertheless, my gracious Lord allowed me to visualize something extraordinary; something that I'm about to reveal to those who believe.

Harvey and I were relaxing at our favorite vacation spot in North Myrtle Beach. The ocean is usually our first choice when we need a break. I have always thought it a mystery to see such a vast amount of water staying in its boundaries as the earth spins around and around. It's a God thing, you know. Since Wendy went to be with the Lord, I have felt closer to her in this setting, as if she and the Lord are out there together in the sky. I seem to talk with the Lord longer and more intensely at the beach.

Harvey had gone to bed, and I was sitting on the deck with my cup of coffee, looking at the sky. The Bible says that God likes to ride the clouds. A very large, fluffy white cloud had appeared and was outlined with a glow of light, almost like a halo. My thoughts were on Wendy, and what she might be doing. As my mind grew deeper in thought, I began to pour

WHY?

my heart out to Jesus, like no other time before. "Lord, I'm thinking about Wendy, and I'm just curious about what she is doing in heaven. I know she is okay with you, Lord. You know how mothers are about their children, and You understand our hearts better than anyone else." I praised Him over and over and thanked Him again for choosing our Wendy to influence others for His kingdom. My conversation with the Lord became so passionate that I felt His presence right beside me. I always try to pray out loud so that Satan can hear and tremble. He cannot read minds as the Lord can, and I wanted him to sweat over my love and faith in God. My prayers were so intense and deeply concentrated that I had no awareness of my surroundings or sounds. It was only the Lord and me. When I stopped praying, all the ocean and surrounding sounds came back, and I felt as if I had been in a trance.

I finally raised my head to the most beautiful nighttime sky. Large, fluffy, white clouds had gathered and were outlined with a glow of light, almost like a halo. As I focused on its unusual beauty, something very mystical caught my attention. "What is this I am seeing?" I asked myself. Focusing more clearly, I could see what looked like angels diving in and out of these clouds. These images were not close enough to see faces, but they were dressed in white and had the form of angels. They seemed to be playfully frolicking in and out of the clouds. They cannot be birds; they are more like human size or larger. I thought I was losing it. I wiped my eyes and looked again, only to see more of the same. Astonished, I ran into the bedroom yelling for Harvey to get up. "Honey, you're not going to believe this; angels are flying in and out of the clouds!" I suppose he thought I was joking with him when he turned over for a more comfortable position. Begging him to come to the deck, seemed to be fruitless. I ran back out making sure I did not imagine things. Lo and behold, they were still there. I cupped my hands around my eyes creating make-believe binoculars. I often do this to shut out other lights and see more clearly. Still, the angels were diving in and out so playfully and energetically. Almost denying my

16: Angels Playing in the Clouds

own eyes and the power of God, I exclaimed, "This can't be for real!" I ran back into the bedroom trying again to awaken Harvey. "Honey, please come outside and witness what I am seeing!" He didn't take me seriously and just refused to get up. Again, I ran back to the deck, looked up; this time they had gone.

Sitting there for a while in wonder, I tried to absorb this vision I had witnessed. I knew I was not dreaming, for I was not asleep. Maybe my eyes were playing tricks on me, I alleged. No, I vividly saw angels in the clouds. Satan is not going to make me doubt this incredible vision given me by the power of the Almighty.

The Bible describes angels as spirits, but God showed me angels in the form that I had pictured them. Wendy is not an angel, she is a saint, who is being served and taken care of by angels as the Bible says.

Still stunned by this awesome site, I sat quietly and mindless for a spell. Turning to the Lord, I asked, "Lord, what does this vision mean? Please help me to understand what you have revealed to me." Immediately, the Lord filled my mind with the answer. "You prayed that I might reveal what Wendy is doing. I sent the playful angels to show you that Wendy is having a magnificent time in heaven. She is happy and worships her Father with the angels. Not only are the angels caring for her, but she is also surrounded by her family and friends that have passed into heaven." I clearly understood that the Lord knew Wendy and her joyful nature.

My heart filled with joy and thankfulness that the Lord Jesus would take His time to reveal these things and to comfort my soul. The Bible talks about having the faith to move mountains. My faith was stronger that night than ever in my life. There was no doubt in my mind that God was going to answer me in some manner. Wendy is safe in His presence, and enjoying the wonders of our promised eternal heaven. After saying thankful prayers, I went to bed with a peaceful heart, and I slept like a baby.

WHY GOD WHY?

Harvey was surprised that I brought this subject up again at breakfast. He remembered my interrupting his sleep with talk of seeing angels. I continued with my excitement about the vision God had given me. Harvey did not question the possibility of seeing unusual things God wanted me to see. He did not know what to say, except, "If you say you saw angels in the clouds, I believe you." I knew Harvey did not experience the same heartfelt emotion without being there.

I didn't tell anyone for a while about this exciting event in my life. I felt it would be hard for others even to understand this vision. My Christian friends and family know that 'faith' is believing in what we cannot see. Only, this was a vision that I did see.

A few months later I signed up for a small Bible study group on Daniel. This study was set up by my missionary cousin, Valerie, who was in the states on a break from the mission field. We met at my Aunt Faye's house with close friends and family. I decided to share my story as we studied about the visions God had given Daniel. None of the other men standing around Daniel could see what God showed him concerning the coming battle. Although they could not see it, they felt it because they ran away with great fear. As things became quiet, I humbly shared my vision with the group. I told them I had tried to wake Harvey from his sleep to witness this great revelation given me. Valerie, very thoughtfully explained, "Violet, had Harvey come to the deck that night, he may not have been able to see what God had allowed you to see. You had so humbly asked the Lord for this."

God answered my prayers through a vision just as he answered Daniel's. Daniel had fasted and prayed for three weeks, and God heard him. I know I am no Daniel, but I had opened my heart many times on that deck, and this night the Lord clearly was there and answered my plea.

God knows our hearts and our thoughts. He understood I needed to see some sign of Wendy's heavenly surroundings. Yes, I believe the Lord put

16: *Angels Playing in the Clouds*

those angels there just for me. How can we place limits on what God is capable of doing? He is the Almighty God of all things and all time, with supernatural powers far beyond our imagination.

I have since told my sister, and a couple of very close friends, about the vision and my special night with the Lord. They believe in the power of God to perform miraculous things. They did not question or doubt my story. Whenever I begin to question that night, the realization grows more vivid in my mind. The song, "My God, is an Awesome God," played in my heart and mind for days after that phenomenal night. God loves us all so very much and wants us to be happy. The Holy Spirit, who indwells us, gives us power when we seek and humbly ask.

Chapter 17
THE LOST BIBLE

Wendy's memory has been kept alive by some unusual events. Her spirit has not only been alive in our hearts and conversations, but also in several incidents from past years. At times, God gifted me with memories that lift my spirit in a calming way. One of those memories nearly jumped out of the box while I was boxing up some old books. One of those books was Wendy's Bible that was once lost.

Several years ago, my sister called to inform me of something very special in the 11 o'clock worship service at our church. "Violet, you are not going to believe this. Dr. Falwell had Wendy's Bible in church today and read the inside cover pages on national television." I was astonished to hear this and thrilled to discover what had happened to her Bible. We had looked for that Bible for a very long time before giving up the search.

Mrs. Vaughan, Tim's kindergarten teacher at Lynchburg Christian Academy, found the Bible. She was so touched by the things written inside that she decided to pass it on to Dr. Falwell. It also touched his heart enough to want to share it with the congregation and the nation. Wendy looked up to Dr. Falwell in a big way. In her eyes, he was the greatest spiritual leader of all time. She always felt special when he spoke and chatted with her in the halls at school.

The presentation page of the Bible was filled in by Wendy and read, "Presented to Wendy Faith Hamilton by her parents, Violet and Harvey, on

WHY GOD WHY?

September 10, 1976." Dr. Falwell read the next page, which Wendy had entitled, 'Thomas Road Baptist and Lynchburg Christian Academy.' On this page, students who had used Wendy's Bible over the years signed their names under the statement: "This Bible was used by…"

Dr. Falwell was slow to speak when he turned and read the next page. Wendy's heading was, 'Salvation Prayer List.' She had written a list of friends and family, just as Dr. Falwell had suggested many times. That prayer list was critical to Wendy, as she sincerely prayed for them daily. Laughingly, he read a few jingle type notes she had jotted down from a few of his sermons:

- "Sin will keep you from this Book, but this Book will keep you from sin."

- "When you come to church, you not only receive a blessing; you are a blessing."

- "When you can't sleep, don't count sheep. Talk to the Shepherd."

- "You can't build a Kingdom without a King."

Tim had used Wendy's Bible while at the academy and probably misplaced it. It must have floated around to different users until Mrs. Vaughan found it years later and noticed that it had belonged to Wendy. Mrs. Vaughn was thrilled to return the long-lost Bible to us. We couldn't thank her enough for her finding it, sharing it with Dr. Falwell, and giving it back to us.

Wendy was full of faith and had a special relationship with her Lord. Even though Wendy is in her new home in heaven, she is still witnessing from her testimony, her words, and her Bible. Her life continues to touch the lives of others. Sharing Jesus was of utmost importance in her heart, and her life exemplified her relationship with Him. God keeps our hearts consoled, knowing that she is in a glorious place and that we will join her one day. Wendy believed in Matthew 21:22 … *"If you believe, you will receive whatever you ask in prayer."*

Chapter 18
OUR SPECIAL BLESSING FROM BRAZIL

As Tim's junior year was coming to an end, I remember how excited he was about moving on to that big senior year and graduation. Unbeknownst to him, that last school year would be a highlight in his life, and not only because of graduation.

One afternoon, a month before the end of his junior year, Tim arrived home completely ecstatic about opening our home to a foreign exchange student. He had removed a picture poster from the school announcement board of this lovely, 16-year-old girl from Rio de Janerio, Brazil. In addition to beauty, Renata Rezende's application letter reflected a spirit that was hard to resist. She seemed to be such a sweet, loving young lady with excitement, spunk, and a mutual hobby interest in playing the guitar. It wasn't her beauty that drew Tim to her. It was as if he had some spiritual connection with this girl he had never met. After a lengthy discussion over dinner, Harvey and I finally agreed to share our home with Renata.

By the next day, Tim had made arrangements for the regional foreign exchange director to interview us at our home. Everything went well, and we were on our way to hosting a stranger for six months. We communicated with Renata and her mother by phone. They spoke fluent English and had the most gracious, yet exciting, air about them. Arrangements were made for Renata to arrive in August before the school year started. She sent pictures, and we talked on the phone many times before her arrival date.

The anticipated day was here as we excitedly rushed to the airport. I was a little nervous when Renata's plane landed. The nervousness immediately vanished upon meeting this warm-hearted, lovely young lady. The first words out of her mouth were, "Dad, Mom, and brother!" Upon meeting Renata, all barriers of a possible communication problem vanished. It was as if she had been a part of our family forever. We were about to load the car with Renata's large size luggage, when she insisted, "No, No, Dad, I will get that!" Wearing a big grin, I leaned over to Harvey and whispered, "She called you Dad." From that day forth, Renata referred to us as Mom and Dad. Our conversation in the car was open and exciting as we shared details about our families and culture.

Tim had arranged a welcome surprise party of family and school friends to greet Renata upon our arrival home. Everyone felt comfortable with Renata as she humbly exhibited appreciation and love for them. She took a short break from the crowd to phone home. She was soft spoken to all of us, but when she started speaking Portuguese to her mom, she spoke with boisterous excitement in her voice. We needed an interpreter to eavesdrop on Renata's conversation with her mother, Elianè.

Renata became a real family member right off the bat. We treated her as if she was our child. She reciprocated with a thankful and loving heart; she had a way of making people around her feel comfortable. We had never seen a more genuine, sincere demeanor than we saw in Renata Rezende. She was a beautiful, highly educated, talented young girl from an affluent family; yet she had, not one pretentious bone in her body. She was thankful for everything (God, friends, gifts, family, rain, snow, school, etc.). She loved life itself. Tim's friends fell in love with Renata instantly. Her good heart and soul rubbed off on all of them.

18: *Our Special Blessing from Brazil*

The rewards we received from this relationship were far more than I could express. Tim and Renata shared a warm special love as if they had always been brother and sister. Elianê noticed the exceptional love between Renata and our family. Both of her parents were pleased with how much we loved her and how we became a real extended family for her.

Renata had originally planned a six-month stay here but quickly requested an additional six-month extension. She would complete her senior year and graduate with Tim. She attended church with us, and we shared our love for the Lord with her. The high school students and teachers also loved our sweet Renata. She taught them, by example, how to care for one another, how to be thankful for the simple things of life and how to be sincere without hang-ups or inhibitions. One day, during school hours, the teacher excused Renata from the class to frolic in the snow. The students laughed while watching her from the window. She had only seen snow from a distance when her father took her to Germany.

Just like my Wendy and Tim, Renata held a special place in her heart for those in need, especially "underdogs." God has given everyone individual talents; Renata's was making people feel very special. Whenever I called her on the phone or arrived home, she would yell "MOM!" with excitement.

We introduced Renata to some of the interesting places like Washington, D. C., New York, the Carolina beaches, and also to William and Mary College where Tim would continue his education.

Flavio and Elianê, Renata's mom and dad, came to the states to see her and visited with our family. Renata's brother, Flavinho, stayed at our home when he came to the states to visit friends. Handsome was an understatement for this young fellow. Flavinho looked Brazilian, while Renata looked more American with her light hair and blue eyes that she acquired from her dad. Two families became one, linked together by this loving young girl.

WHY GOD WHY?

The year passed by so quickly. I dreaded the day when Renata would leave us. I can hear her saying, "Mom, we won't be apart because I will carry you in my heart forever." Renata had hinted that she would like Tim and David to return to Rio with her for a visit. Our large family and a lot of friends from high school went to the airport to bid Renata farewell, and to see Tim and David off.

The local director of foreign exchange affairs said she had never seen such a genuine family relationship as we developed with Renata. This unexplained love was truly from our Lord and will last forever.

How could one exchange student have such a positive impact on, not only our lives, but the lives of the entire community? This exceptional human being touched and lifted every life with whom she came in contact.

Tim & Renata

Chapter 19
NEAR DEATH, AND SO FAR FROM HOME

Tim and Renata had just graduated from high school in June. Tim was to enter The College of William and Mary for the fall semester, while Renata would prepare for medical school in Rio. It was two weeks before Renata was to return to her home in Brazil. Her parents had given their consent for Tim and his friend, David, to come home with Renata for a visit. They were ready for Renata to return home and were happily anticipating seeing Tim again. Rio was an exciting city, but there are also dangerous parts of the city. So the boys were anxious about going.

Renata's family and friends entertained Tim and David as if they were royalty. They introduced them to fantastic places in Rio such as the 130 foot Christ Redeemer Statue on top of Corcovado Mountain, and Sugar Loaf mountain top Utopia. They also went hang-gliding from the mountains to the beach. They enjoyed beautiful beaches and popular sports arenas, and they went to the Rezende's beach house and private club. The love and care the boys received were absolutely incredible.

We missed Tim very much, but we were happy he was having such a great time. He had been phoning us quite frequently, up to the last four days. Harvey and I concluded that the boys were all enthralled with

WHY GOD WHY?

the exciting life in Rio. Anything other than that, Renata would have phoned us.

The next evening, we received a phone call from Teresa, David's mom. Her voice was shaky, and I sensed something was wrong. She said, "Violet, I don't know how to tell you this, but I'm afraid I have bad news from Brazil." My body sent me an alarming distress signal. Not wanting to hear what she had to report, I threw the phone to Harvey, not realizing he had her on the speaker. David had finally telephoned his mom to explain why they had not been in touch for a few days. Teresa relayed his message the best she knew how. "The boys were in a serious car accident four days ago. David's arm was broken in several places with the bone protruding from the skin but…" she hesitated. "What, Teresa, what about Tim?" I anxiously questioned. "Tim is in the hospital with a severe head injury and has been in a sleep coma since the accident. His vitals are getting weaker by the day," Teresa sadly told us. Catching her breath, she continued, "X-Rays showed a massive hematoma on the brain, and Tim will need surgery immediately if his body can withstand the perilous procedure."

David said a rescue truck took Tim to a public hospital where he probably would not have survived a full day. Flavio, Renata's dad, who was head of ophthalmology at a private hospital, quickly had Tim transferred to his hospital, where he would receive the best medical care. He also engaged the most prominent neurosurgeon in Brazil and released Tim into his care.

Once again, we found ourselves helpless when our child needed us. Moving to the deck, I slumped into a chair, and threw my hands up toward heaven. "Oh Lord, Tim is near death and so far from home. Please visit his hospital room and talk with him. I am sure he will feel Your Presence Lord and hear You call his name. So, Lord, I'm leaving it in Your hands, with the faith and trust to thank You now for what you are going to do. And Lord, if it's not asking too much, would You keep a line open that I

19: Near Death, and So Far from Home

might reach You right away?" I heard Him very clearly, "My child, I have always kept a line open to you." I came from the deck feeling much better and ready to be where I was needed.

After talking with Teresa, Harvey phoned our friends in Brazil. Totally embarrassed, Renata humbly tried to explain why they had not called us about the accident. "Oh, Mom and Dad, we are all so sorry! We were so worried and frightened about whether Tim was going to make it. The doctor suggested we pray for a miracle, and that is what we did. But, Mom and Dad, I am so happy to report that Tim has come out of surgery, and he will be okay!" The doctor was as thrilled as the family because it had been touch and go with Tim's vitals. He had to cut a horseshoe opening above Tim's ear, drill through the skull to relieve pressure and liquid from the brain.

Renata then told us the details of the accident. Her brother and a friend had taken Tim and David to the mountains to visit friends. On their return trip down the high mountain, a large truck ran them over a 300-foot ravine, where they flipped several times before crashing to the bottom. It was a miracle that they survived. Tim had the most severe injury, although, they were all hurt and in need of medical care.

Renata said her mom had been sitting with Tim and nursing him night and day since the accident. She was physically and mentally exhausted worrying over Tim and feeling deep guilt that this happened while in their care. Renata also said her mom felt she had aged ten years in the past week. "I know that you want to see Tim. However, my mom has requested that you not come to Rio, now that Tim will be okay. She would not be able to take the pressure right now." It was so very hard to honor her wish. We desperately wanted to be with Tim. Instead, we gave him to Jesus to watch over and comfort.

Talking with Tim a couple of days later lifted my spirits. I knew he was going to be all right, when, in his usual joking manner, told us of his

WHY GOD WHY?

embarrassing moments when Eliané had to hold the urine bottle for him each time he had to use the bathroom. His voice was weak, but when I heard his little chuckle, I felt relieved and felt God's peace.

Tim could not travel for another couple of weeks, but the time quickly passed. Before we knew it, the boys were on their way back home. There were so many people at the airport to greet them and give moral support; I thought they would ask us to leave. Someone yelled, "The plane is here!" We all could feel the excitement in the air.

Harvey grabbed my hand as we moved anxiously toward the door. We watched as the plane emptied out, but there was no Tim and David. Moments later, someone approached the plane with a wheelchair. Nothing could have prepared me for what I was about to see. Tim and David looked as if they had been through a war zone. David had a cast from his fingers to his neck with a metal brace holding his arm from his side. Tim looked like a mummy with his head wrapped in bandages. He had lost a lot of

Tim & David looked as if they were in a war zone

19: Near Death, and So Far from Home

weight and was very frail. I just wanted to hold him in my arms and tell him how much I loved him. I asked his forgiveness for not coming to his side when he needed me. Pictures, hugs, and kisses filled the room, while other travelers looked on. Riding home, I silently thanked the Lord for bringing Tim home safely.

Two weeks later, Tim entered his first year of college. The doctor told us that Tim might have some short-term memory loss along with some moody days ahead. He suggested that Tim wait a semester before starting school. Tim was insistent about starting school with his friend, Keith. Watching Tim display impatience and irritable moods worried me for a while. Thank goodness, time heals and so did Tim. That experience has helped us remember, once again, not to take life for granted. The Lord had more for Tim to do in this life.

Chapter 20
HIS TIMING, NOT MINE

Tim accepted Christ as his Savior at a very young age. His sister, Wendy, led him to the Lord just before her accident. "Why haven't we taken him to be baptized?" I thought about it many times. I mentally punished myself as the subject surfaced over the years with no resolve. I prayerfully posed the question, "Lord, why have we neglected this step of obedience in Tim's life? Please forgive us."

Years later, when Tim was away at college, I phoned him and asked that he pray for Papa Hamilton. From the urgency of my voice, Tim thought Papa might be terminally ill. I assured him that I was just concerned about his spiritual condition. Papa was under conviction, but thought he could not go to heaven because he had fought in the war. Tim loved his grandpa and promised he would pray for him.

Family weekend at the William and Mary campus came before we realized. Our big family went to visit Tim, including grandparents, siblings, nieces, nephews and cousins. We rented seven rooms all lined up beside the pool, as we invaded the Holiday Inn near the campus. We were laughing, snacking and having a great time as we huddled in chairs along the sidewalk outside of our rooms. It looked like the Beverly Hillbillies had come to town.

A couple of Tim's buddies dropped by to share some laughs before leaving for the ball game. Harvey took off to the store for more drinks and snacks.

We were laughing and sharing when Tim addressed the family with an unusual request, "Hey guys, would everyone come into Mom and Dad's room for a few minutes?" We all looked at each other with curiosity as we filed into the hotel room. Since there was a large number of us, we were sitting on the beds, chairs, dressers and the floor. Things got silent as Tim began to speak. His soft voice trembled, and tears welled up in his eyes as he spoke in a somber tone. "I love all of you very much, and I want to share something on my heart that is very important," he softly spoke. "Wendy led me to accept the Lord as my personal Savior when I was a youngster, and I know I will spend eternity in heaven." Tears ran down his cheeks as he sincerely expressed his desire for all of the family to be with him in heaven one day. It was so quiet and chilling that one could hear a pin drop, while tears flowed from every eye in the room. It was evident to me that the Holy Spirit had a strong presence, as He hovered over the room.

"God loved us so much that He sacrificed His Son on the cross for our sins," Tim lovingly continued. "The Bible says, if you put your trust and faith in Jesus Christ, believing that He died for your sins and rose from the grave, you can have eternal life in heaven. Tell Him you believe in who He says He is, and ask Him to forgive you for all your sins and to save you for His kingdom in heaven."

Tim reverently bowed his head and led in a salvation prayer. Lo and behold, Papa Hamilton stood to his feet and told Tim he had prayed and wanted to be in heaven with him. With a shaky voice, Papa asked Tim if he would come home and get baptized with him.

First of all, you would have to know the nature of this grandpa to understand that a miracle just took place. He is quiet around mixed crowds and would never in a million years publically express such feelings unless moved by the Lord Himself.

20: *His Timing, Not Mine*

Harvey, Violet & Tim, while Tim was on break from college

Second, for a young student like Tim to personally share with such sincerity in front of everyone, was definitely a God-thing. The third God-thing was that God's plan was at work. Papa Hamilton did not know that Tim had never gotten baptized. All I could say was, "Praise the Lord!" I knew there were others in the room that needed to do the same.

Harvey had gone to the store and was not there to share this great spiritual moment with Tim and the family. He has always regretted missing such a beautiful, spiritual event. We agreed that it might have been harder for Tim to express himself if he had been there. We don't know, but God does.

Tim came home the next weekend and accompanied his grandpa to a meeting with the church minister. He confirmed that Papa got saved and that Tim also had a personal relationship with the Lord. Tim explained that he did not know why he had never been baptized before this. The minister seemed to know in his heart that the Lord had indeed planned this time for Tim and his granddad to get baptized together.

WHY GOD WHY?

Papa may never have walked that church aisle without Tim by his side. The entire family came and witnessed grandfather and grandson as they got baptized together. Everyone yelled, "AMEN."

Later, while talking with Papa, he shared, "It was all great, except they forgot to heat the baptismal water." We have shared laughs about that over the years.

I now had the closure that I needed with the guilt I had felt for so many years. I realized I had no control over the timing of Tim's baptism. God had planned for him to wait and share this great moment with his grandpa. It was God's perfect timing, not mine.

Papa & Tim after being baptized

Chapter 21
DOUBLE WHAMMY

A parent's worst nightmare is that their child is either sick or in danger. When it comes to your child's safety, no matter how old they are, it is always upsetting. Our Tim has had a few near misses in his short lifetime. The angel that God appointed to watch over him has been very active indeed.

Tim was on his first break from college and still showing some effects of his accident in Brazil. It was nothing bad, but he had mood swings, and he was a little more tired than usual. Some of his close friends, including David and Keith, were also home for break. Arriving home at the same time, was exciting for them. They had made plans for the evening, and Tim was the chauffeur. As always, I told them to be careful on the roads and watch for the other drivers.

Harvey and I settled in to watch television and eat popcorn. We also shared our concerns with one another about Tim's condition. When we moved him into his dorm a few weeks earlier, he was short-tempered and anxious to get things into place. We agreed that he was continuing to show signs of tiredness and restlessness.

It had been a busy day and we both dozed off in our comfy chairs. Around 11 o'clock, we moseyed upstairs and prepared for bed. Usually, I would keep one eye open until Tim arrived home, but after reading for a short while, lights went out, and we both fell into a deep sleep.

WHY GOD WHY?

Suddenly awakened by the screams of two guys in our bedroom sent my heart into adrenalin override. I cannot begin to explain the horror. David and Keith were yelling, "Mr. and Mrs. Hamilton, we've had an accident, and we can't stop Tim from bleeding!" I was still fuzzy and confused from such a wake-up call that my comprehension was slow. Harvey jumped to his feet as the boys related more detail on the way downstairs. Evidently, there had been a light rain, and it made the roads slippery. "Tim's car went out of control and veered through a fence, before dropping head-first into an eight-foot creek embankment," they nervously explained.

I was trying to put my robe on running downstairs, and I nearly fell down the entire flight. Tim was standing in the kitchen covered in blood from head to toe. He was pressing his fingers on an artery in his neck. Each time he released the fingers, blood would shoot across the room. "Oh my goodness, Harvey, get him to the hospital quickly!" I yelled. Since I wasn't dressed, they couldn't wait for me.

I found myself in a familiar situation. I was rushing and praying on the drive to the hospital, and I was afraid of what I might see when I arrived. Of course, my mind had painted a picture of Tim lying in the emergency room in serious trouble. I ran through the emergency doors and asked to see my son. Upon detecting some hesitation, I ordered that they buzz me through to the bay area immediately. I began to have Déjà vu of Wendy's accident as the doors opened to the emergency area abruptly. As I entered the main corridor, I encountered a shocking, double whammy! Not only was Tim lying on a gurney in the hall; my mother was there receiving medical help for her heart. The rescue squad had just rushed her in with hookups all over her. My mom had arrived in time to witness her grandson being rushed in with blood profusely shooting from his neck. That certainly didn't help my mother's condition. I was having an emergency recall with dual family again and didn't know which way to go.

21: *Double Whammy*

While my mother was being checked out, I ran down the hall to see the doctor working on Tim. They were applying pressure on his neck and were preparing to suture the wound to stop the bleeding. In the middle of the procedure, a policeman came in to make sure that Tim was not under the influence while driving. After being satisfied that there was no alcohol involved, the officer left and gave the doctors space to take care of my son. The doctor told us how lucky Tim was to hit the one artery that was a big bleeder, but it was not life threatening. Wow, I believed that bleeding to death was life threatening!

My sisters had arrived at the hospital to care for my mother, giving us the opportunity to take Tim home. Her heart had been racing so hard that it was taking them longer than normal to get it regulated. She was not responding to medications. However, I think Tim became her medication. Once she knew that he was going to be okay, her heart rate slowed a bit helping her body to relax and accept the medications. The doctor prescribed lifetime heart medications and some others for her anxiety.

Guilty thoughts entered my mind as we drove home. Was it too soon after Tim's head injury for him to be driving? It was his first auto accident, where he was the driver. Should we have realized this and forbid him to drive? "Get off that kind of thinking, and be thankful," I scolded myself.

Tim recovered quickly and returned to school in Williamsburg. My mother was admitted to the hospital for a couple of days before being released with more medications to add to her list. We were so thankful that both Tim and my mom recovered and were doing well. It could have been much worse in both situations.

I earnestly prayed for God to help me stop worrying about my family and what might happen next. God replied, "Thank you for trusting me; I'll take it from here."

Chapter 22
ELVIS IS DEAD

"Dad, Elvis is dead! I could see him in two pieces down the tracks and just could not make myself go for him," Tim sadly murmured. Harvey detected a sadness in his voice and it touched him, as he thought about Tim needing his help. The train coming in and out of Williamsburg ran directly behind Tim's house; however, Elvis had never ventured through the shrubs and fence before.

Tim's attachment to Elvis, his black Lab, was more than the usual guy and his dog thing. He had obtained Elvis from the dog pound once he and his friend, Keith, moved from their William and Mary campus dorm to a house nearby. Elvis had already been tagged with his celebrity name before Tim adopted him. It was less confusing to keep his previous name than to train him to respond to a name of Tim's choice. Besides, the name grew on him and Elvis became the fraternity mascot.

Elvis was a great companion for Tim, Keith and many of their college friends who hung out at the house. They roughed around with Elvis and taught him many tricks along the way. Eating holes in all their clothes and furniture was self-taught by Elvis, himself, and became expensive. He loved catching the Frisbee, about 10 feet into the air, then running away with it. Where were all the guys when Elvis needed a bath, or grooming for his show-off days on campus? My Tim just loved that old Elvis dog, and Elvis loved Tim.

WHY GOD WHY?

Harvey had been preparing for the annual Lyons Club fishing trip to Nags Head, which was to begin the following day. Although Tim did not ask him, Harvey felt he should drive to Williamsburg first and take care of the remains of Elvis. He asked his friend, Willis, if he minded detouring to Williamsburg a day early to bury Tim's dog. Willis was a kind friend who would do anything to help others. He was more than happy to accompany Harvey on the trip and help with the dirty deed.

Since losing Wendy years back, we stayed readily available whenever Tim needed us. We kept the road hot from Lynchburg to Williamsburg, not only for visits but for towing cars to and fro which became second nature for us. Harvey once carted a microwave oven on the back of his motorcycle.

Tim was happy to see his dad and Willis pull into the driveway. They exchanged hugs and Harvey introduced Tim to Willis, who had a way of making everyone feel comfortable. The two of them hit it off right away. Before their arrival, Tim had been picking on the guitar, a talent he shared with his dad on many occasions. Willis enjoyed listening to the music, and Tim's spirits lifted as he and his Dad exchanged licks with one another.

Harvey felt it was time to approach the subject at hand, as he brought up the tragedy of Elvis. Tim shared that he couldn't get accustomed to Elvis not running around the house. He especially missed Elvis each time he was leaving. He would yell, "Let's go dog," and Elvis would run for the car.

Harvey and Willis started down the train tracks with shovels in hands. They could see in the distance, the broken figure of a black animal. Tim was correct; the train had divided the body into two parts. Harvey and Willis dug a grave and buried Elvis in a field beside the tracks.

Almost immediately, Tim was talking about the possibility of adopting another dog. When he was a youngster, he always wanted a dog. Hunter was a crazy Irish Setter that ate the neighbor's chickens, the seat off Tim's dirt bike, and a partial seat in Harvey's work van, thus, no more dogs.

Tim laughed and relaxed as Willis told funny stories of his past. After they all had shared time together, Harvey felt they should be moving on toward their destination at Nags Head. Tim thanked them for coming to his aid. As they walked to the car, Tim and Harvey caught up on upcoming events and schedules, then hugged and said their goodbyes.

Tim will always remember his dad coming to his rescue on this sad occasion. Harvey was thrilled that Tim called on him in a tight spot. The love of this father for his son was certainly apparent.

Tim did get himself another dog—a crazy chocolate lab.

Chapter 23
BEYOND MENTORING

Harvey was always full of surprises, but this one caught me off-guard. He asked if I would object to his participating in 'The Big Brothers' program, with the intention of mentoring a young boy. I thought it was time to enjoy some of the fruits of our labor, not start dealing with children again. Tim was away in college, and we were not getting any younger. "You are too old to mentor a young fellow," I projected, out of concern. My negativity was beginning to annoy Harvey.

"Oh, you pal around on the weekends, take them to cultural and social events or just spend time together doing whatever boys do," he explained. With the pressure of our business, involvement in church groups and trips to Williamsburg to visit Tim, I wondered when he would have the time to mentor someone. Harvey had made up his mind. Selfish guilt began to tickle my nerve endings. Harvey wanted to help a young boy in need.

Harvey was given a list of three or four boys from which to choose. He carefully read over each of their credentials, before selecting eight-year-old Brandon, who lived about thirty miles from our home. After meeting Brandon, all I could say was, "Ain't no Ritalin going to hold this boy down." Brandon was a curious livewire who talked non-stop, and with one tone—loud! Brandon lived with his mother and two brothers. Although they had been through some dark days, they were good boys. Their mother raised them with good spiritual and social values. She felt

WHY GOD WHY?

Brandon needed male guidance and attention; therefore, she placed him in the Big Brothers program.

He was smart, but his advanced learning skills had never been delved into. We noticed his exceptional ability in math and technical skills on the computer. We realized he had good potential; however calming down and applying himself would take self-discipline.

All three boys took to Harvey and ended up tagging along many times. Their mother had to remind them that Brandon was Harvey's little brother, not all three. It was hard at times to leave little Jason behind. He was younger than Brandon and did not understand why he couldn't go.

Harvey often brought Brandon, and sometimes all three boys home for eats and social gatherings. I thought Brandon talked non-stop, but the three together jabbered so fast that I couldn't keep up with the conversation. Ryan, the eldest, had aspiring ideas which he shared with great enthusiasm. Jason, the youngest, was not quite as outspoken. He tried many times to express his thoughts, but could not get a word in between Brandon and Ryan. On occasion, Brandon and Jason would stay over for the night. Brandon could eat six eggs, eight slabs of bacon, and a half loaf of toasted bread at one sitting. He always consumed enormous amounts of food, but his high metabolism rate kept his weight to a normal level.

Brandon was aging; he became very attached as his and Harvey's relationship grew stronger. I could see that he loved Harvey, and was growing very close to him. Brandon didn't always allow his brothers to share in the relationship. Harvey spent a lot of time with Brandon, and he went beyond just mentoring, as was required by the Big Brother's program. I thought he might be getting too involved in the family's personal life. Harvey had faith that Brandon could, and would, make something of his life one day. We were aware of the fact that he was bright and showed potential for technical and mathematical skills. We were worried because he was so hyperactive that his mind would not settle down to focus on his classes at school.

Since Brandon's family attended the same church we did, we could always expect Brandon to find Harvey and sit with him. He was already a Christian, and he wanted to do the right things. Brandon was honest, sincere and very likeable, once you got through his chattering.

Brandon became very involved with the church youth program. He went on trips, helped with meetings, and participated in other ways. The leaders took to him right away. Brandon's exuberant personality just grew on you.

Harvey was very patient with Brandon and helped him to learn how to slow down and study. However, at times he would get on your last nerve. You really couldn't offend Brandon, because he was always so enthusiastic that it went right over his head. The relationship between Harvey and Brandon was not the normal Big Brother's relationship. It was a God-thing.

The years went by quickly, and it was hard to believe that Brandon's high school graduation night was here. He was right up there in front, smiling all the way through the program. Sometimes when he smiled, it looked like the cat that was about to eat the mouse. That was Brandon's true smile, not one of self-pride ... just Brandon. That's just how he expressed himself ... happy. His mother was so proud of him, as were we.

Harvey had discussed college with Brandon throughout their years together. He must have comprehended all those discussions. Brandon's brother, Ryan, was a student at Liberty University and tried to influence Brandon to go there. Brandon attempted to apply for LU, but discovered he was unprepared. He was going to need financial aid through grants and student loans, but he wasn't sure how to apply for those and needed assistance. There was a lot more to this than either he or his mother thought. In addition, Brandon was going to need a job for any extra expenses.

WHY GOD WHY?

He stood at the Admissions office, perplexed and down in the mouth, which was not like Brandon. That is when he picked up the phone and called Harvey. Harvey helped Brandon through the long process of application for grants and student loans, as well as the many obstacles of entering college. Brandon qualified for enough assistance and was excited to become a real college student. Until that point, Brandon didn't believe that he would ever get into college.

Brandon spent his first year getting through by the skin of his teeth. He took a job on campus for extra money, in hopes of buying a car one day. His brother, Ryan left school and joined the military. Brandon missed him but tried very hard to move on to the next year. He landed a job with a local manufacturing firm, bought a new car, and found a girlfriend at the same time. Britney was a highly academic VPI and Lynchburg College student. She was a positive influence on Brandon and she not only helped him with his studies, but encouraged him to do his very best in school.

Life, for Brandon, was on the upside. Then, tragedy struck in a big way. His younger brother, Jason had an accident on a four-wheeler and died instantly. Everyone, including church and school, was in a state of shock. It was sad to watch Brandon grieve over his loss. We understood his pain, and we knew what he was going through. He continued to contact Harvey whenever he needed to talk with someone. Harvey delicately listened to every word, with empathy and love.

Brandon's academic ability finally kicked in. He put his mind to school work and also worked very hard on his job. He was excellent with math and took jobs tutoring young students around town. He then became a soccer director and coached Little League teams throughout the city. Brandon was growing up and heading in the right direction. Harvey and Brandon remained brothers throughout college years.

Finally, college graduation! Just like in high school, Brandon smiled so proudly that he could not hide his excitement. Brandon had the tenacity to fight hard for his education. There were times when my faith in his future was dim. However, Harvey and I prayed for him and had faith that the Lord would take care of Brandon. He joined the Navy as an officer and a gentleman. He fought hard and did well at boot camp, then set sail for months before his first leave. Britney took a position teaching physics in a town near Brandon's base in Norfolk.

Brittney and Brandon had their future all planned out, including marriage date—a year away— after his tour and after she felt secure in her job. The big day of tying the knot finally came. Brandon was like a little kid who could never hide his expressions. They requested that our grandson, Wyatt, be the ring-bearer. With the help of her family, Britney had planned for the event to take place directly after Brandon finished his tour of duty at sea.

It couldn't have been a more beautiful wedding. The children, grandchildren, Harvey and I sat together anticipating getting a glimpse of Brandon, Britney, and Wyatt. I kid you not, if I thought Brandon displayed that kid-like grin before, this topped them all. As usual, he was grinning from ear to ear all the way down the aisle, with that same innocent, 'I made it' grin. The reception was beautiful and well planned. We were so proud of Brandon's accomplishments.

Brittney, Brandon and their two daughters are sharing a wonderful life together. Brandon has also completed his master's degree. We don't worry about Brandon anymore. The Lord has taken care of him and had a plan for his life's journey the whole way. Brandon continues moving in the right direction with God. Harvey's time invested in Brandon was rewarding for both.

Chapter 24
A SPONTANEOUS VACATION WITH ADVENTURE

Out of the blue, Harvey decided that we were going to Key West, Florida. He was so excited about this trip, but I was nervous about his urgency to leave in the next few days with little time to prepare. We had heard good things about the Keys from friends. Tim was in college, the business was going very well, so he thought it was a perfect time to go. I don't believe we had ever taken a two-week vacation before. When we previously planned our trips in advance, things would come up with the business, and we would invariably cancel our trip.

A local travel agency responded quickly to our needs and completed our package in a few hours. Ready or not, we were off on our first leg to Miami, where we would catch the commuter flight to Key West. The commuter was late leaving, putting us there very late in the evening. Upon arrival, we learned that our luggage did not arrive with us. They assured us that they would deliver it to the hotel when it arrived. I was upset, but Harvey didn't pay it any mind. He had spotted Jimmy Buffet's airplane. To him, that was more exciting than our luggage.

WHY GOD WHY?

We arrived at our hotel on the beautiful Gulf side of Key West. Surprise number two, the hotel, inside and out, was surrounded by building equipment, bricks, supplies and men working everywhere. It looked as if they were in the midst of building this place. You would think that a travel agency would know these things. "Honey, is this where we are to spend our vacation?" I asked frantically. The attendant at the check-in desk apologized for the disturbance and did not hesitate to confess that they had opened, but were not quite finished building. We explained that our luggage would be delivered from the airport, probably tomorrow morning.

I was looking forward to looking out my window to see the ocean and the sunrise. Sadness was written over my face when we were assigned a side room with no ocean view. My view was just an old garage building and uncut grass. Surroundings are a big part of the vacation for me. Harvey could see disappointment all over my face. He suggested that we get some sleep and check on things in the morning. I wanted this vacation to be my utopia. Without luggage, I had no night clothes to relax in so I decided to shower in the morning and went to bed. It took quite a while, but I finally drifted off into la-la land. Shocked by pounding on the door at 3:00 a.m., we jumped out of bed and slipped our clothes back on. It was the bellboy with our luggage. We were upset that they would wake us up in the middle of the night instead of waiting until morning.

Morning came too quickly, and my body was not ready for the day nor was my brain. "A good shower might wake me and get me excited for the day," I thought. Half asleep, I jumped into the shower, before turning the water on. Usually, I test the water before getting into the shower. Thinking that new plumbing should give a gentle flow of water, I flipped the handle wide open. That over-sized faucet blew off the tub with amazing force and hit my shin so hard that my screams could be heard throughout the hotel. The force of the blow made an indention in my leg, and the

24: A Spontaneous Vacation with Adventure

veins popped out like large blood clots. Swelling began immediately. However, the skin did not break, so I was positive I was going to live. Harvey came running to see what had happened. He phoned the front desk and received an immediate response. The manager investigated and found that the builders had not connected the faucet to the tub with screws. The thing was, our room had been checked off as complete when it shouldn't have been. I was left with a permanent sink-hole and bubbled up blood vessels to remember the vacation.

Consequently, we received first class treatment and were awarded one of the best rooms on the oceanfront. My leg was very sore, but I was much happier where I could view the ocean and watch the huge passenger ships dock. "Lord, you sure have an interesting way of making me see the bright side of things," I uttered in low key.

That first evening, while strolling through the main street, we found Jimmy Buffet's restaurant, Margaritaville. Harvey liked Buffet's music, and we hoped this would be one of the nights he would show up and entertain everyone. We heard that no one ever knows when he will be around. We ate very slowly and drank iced tea until I thought I would float away. We were hoping this would be one of those nights Buffet would appear. Harvey, being a musician himself, would have loved to be entertained by a professional. The next day, we found out that Jimmy did show up, and it was about thirty minutes after we left. We had just missed him.

It is customary in Key West to celebrate the going down of the sun each evening. From our balcony, we could watch all the festivities on the dock next door where the big cruise ships docked. Bands played island music, magic tricks were performed, and dancers danced, along with vendors selling food. As is the custom in the Keys, when the last tip of sun dipped out of sight, roaring cheers came from the crowd along with the celebration music. This tradition went on every evening at sundown.

WHY GOD WHY?

We did not have much of a beach on the Gulf side of Key West. If you wanted to go to the beach, they would use a boat to take you out to a small island covered with rocks. It was not the kind of beach I expected from the Keys. Trying to make the best of it, Harvey and I decided to rent bikes and hit the tennis courts a few blocks away. Every day we played tennis and rode bikes all around Key West. At dusk, we would sit on a park bench, sip on a milkshake and listen to a great blues band perform on the upper porch of a quaint old Charleston like home. Harvey was in his element with a keen ear to the music. The filtered light of the moon glistened on the lit up trees, and the stars twinkled as if they were happy. As long as Harvey was listening to the music, I could lay my head on his lap, and he would rub my back, which I loved.

Today, I was extremely excited to take a tour boat. Schools of beautiful fish and some shark glistened against the filtered sun rays from above. This vacation was the most relaxing one we had ever taken. The hotel pool area had many palm trees and flowers of many bright colors to view. A waterfall at the end of the swimming pool soothed our ears as we dozed in the sun and felt the ocean breezes.

We rented a car and drove up through the Keys for one long day. A nasty storm came up on the return trip. There is only one two-lane road, lined with the Gulf on one side and the Atlantic on the other. I felt uneasy due to the high winds and downpour of rain. I asked Harvey if he thought this narrow road had ever flooded. He could not answer, but suggested that I enjoy the storm and not worry about it … Right!!!

The last day was bright and sunny, with a beautiful blue sky and white clouds floating to the north. Harvey wanted to surprise me by taking us to a spot of incredible beauty. There was a high-rise Holiday Inn on the southern shore of Key West. Looking from the roof of the hotel, we could see the Gulf to the right, the Atlantic Ocean to the left,

24: A Spontaneous Vacation with Adventure

and straight ahead where they met. I was speechless as I slowly gazed completely around these southern waters. The south side was like being on a cruise with water all around, and the northern side displayed the beautiful streets lined with Charleston structured houses. With the trees in between, it was like looking at a still painting in a museum. What a fantastic vacation memory from the Keys.

Our flight back to Miami, and then to our layover in Charlotte was uneventful. We waited at the end of a corridor, where we would board the airplane parked right outside the window. While Harvey was reading, I was listening to a conversation taking place on the airport network phone just below us. An airplane mechanic was saying things like, "I have tried everything, and I don't know how to fix the problem."

My eyes followed him through the window, to our designated plane just outside. He and two other mechanics worked very aggressively on the problem. Moments later he came back in, dialed the phone again and said, "I'm looking at the book and cannot find a link to the problem." Then he said, "Okay, I will try again." That little fellow came in a couple more times with questions to his colleague on the other end of the phone. I am not comfortable flying as it is, let alone after hearing this conversation about our plane having a mechanical problem. "Harvey, did you hear that conversation over there?" I asked. "No, I am reading, and I am not as nosey as you," he replied hastily.

Within moments, the intercom announced the boarding of our flight to Lynchburg. By this time, I was extremely nervous about flying this particular aircraft. Against my gut feelings, I took Harvey's hand as we entered the plane, only to find that we could not sit together. These planes were small, and seats were sparse. I shared a seat in the first row with a young man who looked about as anxious as I did. Harvey had to take a seat on the back row.

WHY GOD WHY?

There was only one attendant, who looked very jittery. She strapped herself into a seat facing us, just a few feet away. The plane had a lot of rattles, and I wondered if it would stay together until we leveled off. A few minutes into the flight, the captain announced that everyone should stay in their seats with seatbelts fastened. Several minutes later, the captain made another announcement, "Ladies and gentlemen, we seem to have a problem with the airplane and it doesn't look too good." I'm not kidding, the attendant verbally projected with a horrified voice, "I just knew it, I just knew it!" If I wasn't scared to death already, I certainly was then. Everyone was quiet as the voice of the captain came back to update us. He apologized for the inconvenience and explained that we would have to return to Charlotte and fix the problem. Wow, I witnessed them fixing problems an hour before takeoff … What now?

No one was sure whether we would get back to Charlotte. I was not the only one apprehensive about our situation. When the wheels touched down, I gave a sigh of relief. We vacated the aircraft and went inside the terminal. They told us that our plane would need some work, and we would be boarding again shortly. Anyone that knows me, and my fear of flying, could guess at that point what my reaction was going to be. "Harvey, I am not going to get back on that aircraft. I am not!" Harvey thought I was silly. However, he knew that it would be an all-out war trying to convince me to re-enter that plane. They called for boarding again, but I just was not confident in the aircraft or their repair job.

We found a hotel for the night and rented a car the next day to drive three hours' home. Maybe I did not have the faith I should have. However, if you have a couple of danger signs, you should take them to heart. Right? All Harvey kept talking about was all those people who took the flight were already home in their comfortable beds, safe and sound.

It was a wonderful vacation, right up to the last day. One thing is for sure, "If you want to go anywhere and not have a dull moment, just travel with Harvey and Violet," say our friends. God is not done with us yet; I'm still a work in progress. The trip was good for us to reconnect and spend some necessary "us" time together. Yes, I got scared about the plane. Yes, my faith had grown dim, and I did not trust enough to get back on that aircraft. However, I never lost my faith in God.

Chapter 25
TWO SUPER GENES UNITE

There has always been a circle of very close and dedicated friends, both male, and female surrounding Tim. College life at William and Mary was no exception; friends gravitated together as if they were family. Keith, a good friend from years past, was Tim's roommate and an integral part of their group of mutual friends.

Tim dated on various occasions, but nothing serious developed from his relationships. Four years passed very fast and graduation was just a few months off. Out of the blue, we received a couple of suspicious pictures from Tim with no explanation. A cute, petite young lady, smiling from ear to ear, was standing close by his side. She was one of Tim's peers I had previously seen in pictures, but not with Tim. He didn't mention anything serious to us, but continued dating this girl. I heard through the grapevine that their friends thought they were a perfect match. I was very anxious to meet this young student who was filling a special place in my son's life.

We finally met Laura at graduation. We also met her brother Matt, her parents, Lyle and Mary Ann and grandmother, Pauline (Polly) at the graduation events. Harvey and I, along with two other parents hosted a cookout, honoring our graduating sons. A beautiful cottage overlooking the James River, accessed by a ferry ride, was a perfect setting. Family members, college friends, and others, including Laura and her family, were invited to the celebration. Knowing I had to put on my good hostess hat, I greeted everyone, brought out food, and set up tables.

It was a beautiful day, and the cookout was a huge success. Everyone seemed to be enjoying their time together, young and old. I grew tired of trying to be the perfect hostess, and I didn't want to look too pretentious. Feeling famished, I finally got a plate of food and plopped into a chair under the center tent. Immediately, my chair collapsed under me; down I went yelling like a lunatic, and my food went flying into the air all over anyone near me. To say I was totally embarrassed would be an understatement. Of course, it attracted the attention of everyone at the affair. That was the first impression the Lacy family had of Tim's mom.

After graduation, Laura went on a trip across the country with a few close roommates. They enjoyed working dude ranches, and seeing the sights as they traveled to their destination. There wasn't much that they didn't do before arriving to visit a college roommate who lived in Oregon.

On the other hand, Tim did not have the luxury of a vacation or relaxation. Time constraints forced him to accept a job offer that he could not refuse in Northern Virginia.

Tim was missing Laura very much, and decided he needed to do something about it. He was a very bright fellow and displayed his smarts when he considered Laura Elizabeth Lacy as his future bride. Adding her exceptional intelligence and personality to Tim's, and you have two 'Super Genes' uniting.

Tim wrote, "You're All I need," a beautiful love song for Laura. He transferred it to sheet music and asked his dad to help him create a soundtrack. The song touched me as I listened to Tim sing along with the music. Who would have guessed? His plan was to travel to Oregon and surprise Laura by presenting the song in person, followed by a marriage proposal.

25: *Two Super Genes Unite*

Secretive plans were beginning to develop between Laura's traveling buddies and Tim. The girls were to bring her to a local pub where they had live music and karaoke entertainment. Tim decided to take only the soundtrack and leave his guitar home. A couple of the girls picked him up at the airport and drove him to the pub. He quickly went into action, setting up and testing his music on their sound system. Everything seemed to work okay, but he was still nervous and excited at the same time.

The girls finally arrived and took their seats front and center. Without warning, Tim appeared on stage with a mike in his hand. Laura was completely caught off guard, which is unusual for her. Tim turned on the equipment, only to find that his soundtrack was not working. "Oh my, what am I going to do?" he thought. He tried it again, but to no avail. As Tim would, he proceeded to sing from his heart, and without music. By this time, Laura was in shock mode. With anticipation, the girls excitedly looked on as Tim walked over to their table, still singing. He went to his knees and asked Laura to marry him. An immediate "YES!" penetrated the room. The redness finally faded from Tim's face and the two shared a fantastic evening together.

Tim singing to Laura at their wedding

Tim flew back to his D.C. job, while Laura took a bus to another state to catch a connecting flight back home. To tell you that some crazy person ran into her bus, shot at them and held them up would sound incredible. It's true, but I will save it for another time.

Oatlands Plantation was a perfect venue for their wedding. The arrangements, the weather, and large turnout were more than we could have hoped for. Family members and friends filled the wedding garden as if they were bouquets of flowers. Renata, our special adopted daughter from Brazil, flew in to share this wonderful occasion with us. Many college friends shared their support at the wedding, and several participated.

The honeymoon in Spain and France was terrific for Tim and Laura. They never meet a stranger regardless of the location. Communicating with the locals wasn't too hard, considering Laura spoke Spanish and Tim brushed up on his French. They didn't miss a thing as they filled their days with exciting adventures, that only they would attempt.

Stand aside when God is moving two people together, and into His plan.

Chapter 26
WE'RE GOING TO CRASH!

Harvey is an excellent pilot, whom I trust more than any other. We flew many times to visit clients, and on vacations, but flying has always made me nervous. I could not conquer my fear of flying or not having control. Commercial flights were different from our private aircraft—less shaking, two pilots, and two engines. To be honest, I don't like flying in any airplane.

Before Harvey moved up to a twin-engine, our little six-seater had completed many missions successfully, and many times without me. At times, Harvey reminded me of how much I would miss being with the family on exciting trips, as he tried to coerce me along. The sad thing is, however, I have waved goodbye to my family many times.

This flight was one of two experiences that justified my fear of flying. Both flights revealed a vision of my life floating in front of me. This time, Harvey, Tim, Laura and I were flying to Rio de Janerio to attend our previous exchange student Renata's graduation from medical school as a full-fledged doctor.

As I thought about the twelve-hour flight ahead to Brazil, I was somewhat nervous, especially since the aircraft acted up on the takeoff from Dulles. Tim reminded me to keep the faith that I had taught him in previous years. It was all worth it when we flew over the ocean and around Rio. The huge, well known Christ statue on Corcovado Mountain, was towering well above everything else. Many in the airplane were completely astonished by the beauty.

The visit to Brazil and sharing with Renata's family, was more than we could have ever expected. They had made our reservations in this grand hotel called, Ipanema. The staff treated us as they would royalty. A large fruit and cheese tray was waiting to greet us in our room. The ocean views were as far as the eye could see, and the mountains were unusually shaped. From the rooftop pool area, we could see the Christ statue and the famous Sugar Loaf Mountain.

Renata's family went overboard to create a memorable stay in Brazil. We will remember this trip in our hearts forever as we shared Renata's success as she became a full-fledged doctor. Her parents planned a celebration afterward that we all attended.

The return trip back to the States seemed to be faster than the one to Rio. We landed back in Dulles, kissed the children goodbye and boarded our plane to return home to Lynchburg. The control tower gave Harvey permission to taxi out to

"I'm a doctor," yells Renata

26: *We're Going to Crash!* 141

the runway. Many planes were ahead of us for takeoff, and that allowed me time to worry about the bumpy flight over the mountains. Harvey had checked the weather between Dulles and Lynchburg and received a clear report. My heart raced as the voice from the tower directed, "856 Sierra Charlie, you are cleared for takeoff." It always gives me goosebumps when Harvey revs the engine while traveling down the runway at a high rate of speed. My stomach gets butterflies on the liftoff. I usually wish my flight away anticipating the landing at the other end.

It was an uneventful flight until about twenty-five miles outside of Lynchburg. "Oh no!" I loudly exclaimed. We watched a mist of white ice quickly forming over the windshield, totally blocking forward vision. I was not aware until this moment that we had no de-icer. Non-visual flying would be no problem considering Harvey is an IFR-rated pilot who can fly using instruments. However, instrument rating or not, he must be able to see the runway to land this thing.

When I get nervous, I chatter, and this was no exception, "Harvey, what are we going to do? How are we going to land? Do you have a plan?" The control tower in Lynchburg finally answered our call, and I was still chattering like a chipmunk. The air traffic controller's first question was, "How many people do you have on board?" Harvey replied, "Just my frightened wife, sir. Please turn up the runway lights as high as they will go. I have white ice and no visual for landing."

The storm expected for 6:00 p.m. fooled everyone when it moved in at 1:30 p.m. It was windy, cloudy and snow was beginning to fall. By this time, I had made myself sick from trying to figure how we would land. "Where is your faith?" I asked myself. I didn't get an answer back. "How are we going to land, Harvey?" We usually see the runway as we cross over the mall, but not this day. "Harvey, are we going to crash? I can't see the ground or the runway. "Honey, be quiet! Prepare yourself for landing, please!" He was in a tight spot trying to maneuver the plane sideways to see out the side window and forward again. He was trying to avoid having the runway meet us before we could see it. "856 Sierra Charlie, this is the tower, please respond," we heard. "This is 856 Sierra Charlie on final approach," responded Harvey. "856 Sierra Charlie, lights on high; good luck," were the comforting words from the tower—then silence. The fog also added to the icy condition. I still could not see the runway as Harvey continued his strange approach, sideways and front again. I gripped the seat for a tight hold as we descended.

Harvey was hoping to see at least dim lights on the runway, but nothing yet, and he told me to brace myself. I had no training for this type of emergency. My jaw was so tight from the tension that I thought my teeth would crack. Just as we crossed the bypass, we could see lights very faintly, but still could not see the actual ground. The plane was twisting back and forth from the high winds. Then Harvey straightened it up and gave me the old, "This is it, hold on!" Suddenly … B-U-M-P … as the wheels touched the ground for a safe landing. All I could say was, "Thank you, Lord! Thank you Lord!" And I should not forget to credit my Harvey for his proficient flying skills. I think he secretly enjoyed the drama.

Words echoed from the tower, "856 Sierra Charlie, nice job on the landing." I felt like we were starring in one of those movies where everyone in the tower claps after an emergency landing. The controller asked us to take the next exit ramp and wait for the lead truck to guide us to the terminal. When we finally came to a stop, we rested back in our seats and remained immobile for a few minutes before exiting the aircraft.

This flight did not help my fear of flying one bit. Harvey, with his usual comment, reminded me that it is always safer in a plane than in a car. As I always say, "But, you can pull over in a car."

He realized he was fighting a losing battle. However, we stopped and gave thanks to our Lord for watching over us and bringing us safely home.

Chapter 27
FROM A CRUISE TO THE EMERGENCY ROOM

We had just returned from a wonderful cruise to the Cayman Islands. Deda, Johnny, Harvey and I had the greatest time sailing and touring together. Since our children were babies, the four of us had shared some amazing times. Harvey took advantage of everything, including scuba diving in the beautiful Grand Cayman waters.

The four of us had mixed sentiments as we witnessed the extraordinary and the unusual. We were either in stitches, astonished, or saddened by situations and events of the trip. We laughed at funny sights and were overwhelmed with God's beautiful creations. Toward the end of the trip, we witnessed a heartbreaking tragedy for a couple on the cruise. The husband had a heart attack and was enduring a pretty long wait before a helicopter retrieved both of them. Many of us were on the top deck watching the helicopter hovering over the ship. A basket was lowered from the aircraft. The wind made it difficult to maneuver the basket. Finally, both wife and husband were successfully lifted up and swept away.

We wished for an extension on this vacation that was shortly coming to an end. When we returned home, Harvey and I were immediately back to business as usual. "Honey, isn't it time to retire yet?" I asked. I received no return comment.

WHY GOD WHY?

Just like clockwork, Harvey resumed his daily tennis games at a local club. Six o'clock every morning was the scheduled time. Today was not only a wake-up to exercise, but a wake-up call for his life. Fifteen minutes into the match, Harvey became very ill, and his face was grayish/white. The clerks at the club gave him a couple aspirins.

Harvey's ride dropped him off, and I was surprised that Harvey would be returning home so soon. Then I heard a weak, shallow voice call for my help. "Harvey, what is wrong with you?" I yelled as I hurried down the steps. Frightened to death at the sight of him, I ran to help lower him to the floor. He was white as a ghost, very limp, and could hardly talk. I wondered why someone did not help him into the house. "I'm sick, and my chest feels tight," he exclaimed. He said that someone had given him two aspirins at the club.

Harvey rarely gets sick, so this was beginning to scare me. When he began to complain about the pain in his arm, I ran to the phone to call our doctor. He was asking me questions that I could not completely answer. He yelled, "For goodness sake, Violet, take the phone to Harvey!" The answers from Harvey were very weak and shaky. He dropped the phone to the floor. Tom said, "Get him to the hospital quickly, or better still, take him up to my office." The office was only three miles away. The staff would be getting there and could check him out.

It was a task trying to get Harvey to the car. That was the longest three miles I had ever driven. Harvey sat in the car while I checked the door to the doctor's office. It was locked, and the receptionist inside was yelling, "We're not open yet!" I kept knocking on the door until someone opened it. I told them that the doctor had told me to bring Harvey in. "He may be having a heart attack!" I abruptly announced. They quickly placed him on a table for observation. A practical nurse and one doctor had come in early. An EKG immediately confirmed that Harvey was into an active heart attack.

27: *From a Cruise to the Emergency Room*

More doctors showed up and tried unsuccessfully to get an IV running. Harvey's veins had collapsed and would not take the fluid. The room was full of staff, so I stepped into the hall to phone my sister, asking her to come. I felt helpless and stepped back into the room just as Harvey projectile vomited all over everyone working with him. "Somebody better do something, or he is going to die right there on the table!" I thought. "Call the rescue squad!" the doctor directed the nurse. Three hours had now passed since Harvey became ill.

They were working on Harvey in the squad truck while I nervously sat up front with the driver. My sister, Sheilla was following in her car. When we reached the hospital, Dr. Thomas Nygaard, Head of Cardiology, was waiting at the emergency room door. He started running and pulling the gurney down the hall, while at the same time asking me questions. Harvey seemed to be fading and time was of the essence. It was hard for me to keep up with them as we ran to the OR. I grabbed Harvey's hand when we approached the double doors, where I was left behind. Collapsing in a chair, I cried uncontrollably. "Lord, I am so full of fear, please forgive me." We just returned from a wonderful cruise and straight into an emergency situation. "Lord, it's all happening so fast, and I can't handle it without You close by my side." Sheilla and a couple of others had parked and finally joined me in the waiting area. I was so upset and didn't know what to expect. Harvey had been my life, and I needed him.

The procedure took twenty minutes. The doctor inserted a stint into the 100 percent blocked artery that caused his heart attack. I could not believe it was over so fast. Shockingly, he added that Harvey needed a six-way bypass, and it would be best to perform this immediately. The doctor scheduled the surgery for the next morning.

Laura's father got in touch with Tim and Laura, who were on a trip to Nebraska. They immediately caught a flight back to Virginia to be with us. Our family, friends, and pastors helped to console us and offer their sup-

WHY GOD WHY?

port. The doctor had explained the complexity of stopping the flow to the heart and moving over to a machine while doing the bypass. These were tense times, and I did not know what to expect. My comfort level changed when Laura and Tim arrived; much quicker than we expected.

The next morning, I was very apprehensive during our consultation with the doctor. It was his duty to explain all possibilities with this complex operation. We all kissed Harvey goodbye as they moved his bed toward the surgery unit. Many friends and family gathered around to await the outcome and to support us. When the operation was complete, the doctor communicated the procedure process and Harvey's progress. Tim placed his arm around my shoulder. "Everything went well," the doctor said. I felt like a ton of bricks had been lifted off of me. Tim and I were allowed to go in to see Harvey when he began to awaken. The nurse explained that until he could wake up completely, and breathe on his own, he must stay hooked to the breathing machine. I was thankful, but couldn't stand to see him in that condition. He would go in and out of sleep trying desperately to breathe on his own. Harvey was about to panic thinking he could not breathe. The nurse kept telling him that a machine was breathing for him, and until he could breathe on his own, they could not disconnect. Harvey was trying to talk and couldn't get out what he wanted to say. Tim started talking with him in hopes of getting his mind off the situation. I couldn't bear to see Harvey in that condition and had to leave the room. Tim stayed right by his dad's side, keeping him calm for over two hours. He continued to talk and coax Harvey until he could finally breathe on his own. He had Harvey up and walking down the hall when I returned. "Lord, you did it again," I whispered in my prayers.

Dr. Nygaard made us feel special each time he checked on Harvey. He was the kindest, most wonderful doctor we had ever met. It was as if Harvey was his only patient. He took time explaining the condition, listening to concerns and always asked about everyone in the family.

27: *From a Cruise to the Emergency Room*

Harvey tried to do all the right things for a quick recovery. I had already returned to work while Harvey recouped at home. Being a pilot, he had to pass many tests and obtain permission from the Federal Aviation Administration to continue flying. All of Harvey's doctors knew that flying was a priority on his list, and went to great lengths to assure that he got reinstated as an aircraft pilot.

Dr. Nygaard concluded that stress probably had a lot to do with his heart attack. To our surprise, Tim and Laura decided to give up their jobs, sell their house and move to Lynchburg to help with our business. They showed their love when they altered their life's journey. Tim had advanced far in the technical field and had leadership experience to bring to the table. Harvey and I were exceedingly overjoyed when we heard this great news.

We would get to watch our future grandchildren grow and share in their lives with them living nearby. Another blessed announcement was from Laura; she was expecting our first grandchild.

Tim, after a few years at the helm

Time has passed, and we now have three grandchildren. Tim and Laura have been so pleased to raise them in the Lynchburg area. Sometimes we ask God—Why? Why do things happen the way they do? I could not think of anything greater than having our children and grandchildren near us. God's plan for us is so much greater when we let go and let Him guide.

Chapter 28
THE PROPELLER IS GOING!

That flight from Dulles, with iced windows, did not hold a candle to the one that halted my flying days. We had planned another trip to the beach, and of course, Harvey insisted on flying. Deda and Johnny were excited about accompanying us on this trip. I tried every excuse in the book to convince Harvey of the need to drive instead of flying. "Come on Honey, the weather looks great, and you know that an hour by air is so much better than six hours by ground," argued my determined husband. I convinced myself that the trip would seem fast from all of our chitchat in the back. Deda and I always filled our trips by bringing each other up-to-date on our families, etc. It never entered my mind that March can sometimes be the windiest month of the year.

The flight down was very calm, with clear visibility to view all the great sights. In fact, it was so smooth that I relaxed and released my grip from the armrests. Hearing Harvey contact the tower controller, indicated that we were approaching the coastal area. We spotted the intercoastal waterway and knew the next sight would be the breathtaking horizon of the ocean. It always seemed to come up and meet the clouds. Deda and I discussed the miraculous creation made by an awesome God. Harvey and Johnny were consciously looking for other aircraft as we crossed over into

WHY GOD WHY?

Myrtle Beach air space. "Get ready for the landing," Harvey informed us, as he took his final approach. I like to hear the tower announce, "clear to land," much better than, "clear to take-off." As always, when we touched down, I gave my usual sigh of relief.

The few days we had at the beach were glorious, but went by much too fast. It was nearing time for the return flight and just thinking about it made me nervous. Harvey checked the computer for weather conditions, and everything seemed okay. "Maybe just a little wind," he offered. I have flown in the wind before, and I don't like it. I asked him several times, "Honey, did you check for weather all the way home?" We finally began to board the aircraft, and I thought to myself, "Why am I doing this again? I need to give this fear of flying to God and have the faith that all will be in His hands."

Things are always a little bumpy; especially when we take off or land and when we enter large clouds, so it didn't worry me that much. The first fifteen minutes seemed to be somewhat bumpy; however, I gave it no mind. Deda and I were having our usual conversation about some funny old times. As we approached the Raleigh air space, the wind suddenly picked up with a little more force. "Deda, I don't like this bumping in the winds, how about you?" I softly muttered. "Neither do I, but everything will be okay," she replied. When I get nervous, I ask Harvey questions about the conditions in hopes of receiving positive feedback. "I think it will be a little windy the further north we go," was a reply I did not want to hear. Our plane only had one engine and one propeller.

It wasn't long until things changed for the worse. The wind grabbed our airplane, lifted it fifty feet into the air, and then dropped it fifty feet. The plane was being tossed around as if it was a toy. I thought we were falling out of the sky and screamed out as I looked over to see Deda's reaction. She was trying to be brave, but I could see some shock on her face. Before I could say anything to Harvey, the wind hit us again, and again, throwing

28: *The Propeller Is Going!*

us all over the sky. Deda and I were holding on for dear life as we bounced up to the ceiling and back. Johnny was giving it that old male, macho silence. Honestly, I truly thought, "This is it for us."

I watched Harvey intensely trying to hold the plane on course. "Harvey, turn around, go back to Raleigh!" I shouted. The headwind was so forceful that it seemed like we were suspended in mid-air and not moving at all. This pitiful little plane was working itself to death. "Harvey!" I yelled again, "The propeller is going to break off, I know it is." He told me he was flying the speed necessary for these types of wind forces. "Sit back and keep calm," he gently directed.

If I ever thought things couldn't get worse, I was wrong. Things got worse—a lot worse. Deda got silent as if she might be praying. With both hands, we were trying to hold ourselves in the seat. I kept thinking of that propeller breaking off, or maybe the wings. The wind seemed to be in control as we continued to be twisted in different directions. The plane kept pushing very hard. However, we should have been in Lynchburg a long time ago. I know it sounds silly, but I remembered the children's story of the train that said, "I think I can, I think I can, I know I can, I know I can." Then it hit me, "It is not I that can, it is God that can," and I knew He could, and would. That made me calm down and control myself.

The further north we traveled, the worse the winds were. We were about twenty miles outside of Lynchburg, our destination when Harvey called in for landing conditions. They informed us that a plane had just landed with an incident because of the crosswinds and to be very careful. My heart was racing a little, but I said nothing. Harvey is my excellent pilot, and God is in control. At the third mile mark, Harvey keyed the mike, "Confirm clear to land." We received a clear-to-land confirmation.

The wind was swinging us from side to side as we went down for the approach. It felt as if we were in a swing. The crosswinds did catch us, but Harvey held on to the centerline. "Hold on, here we go," were the

WHY GOD WHY?

next words from Harvey's mouth. Our stomachs churned when the plane sank just before touchdown. It was a big relief to hear the wheels touch the ground. "Yes!" Deda and I screamed. "We're safe at home from another one of our adventures."

Thumbs up

Harvey did admit that this was the worst wind he had ever encountered. Once again, Deda announced, "Another adventure. It is never a dull trip when traveling with our best friends." Johnny finally spoke, "A piece of cake, right Harrrrv?"

Chapter 29
THE GRANDFATHER

Our lives consisted of several life changing tragedies, but through it all God brought us out of the deepest pit and took us to the highest mountain. Only God can give and take away the way that He does. Even though we had previously lost our daughter, Wendy, and nearly lost our son, Tim, God knew just the way for us to see His love and bring new blessings into our lives.

Harvey announced, "I want them to call me Grandfather, just like in the movie, 'Heidi,'" "Them who?" I asked with a grin on my face. Harvey looked at me with a smile and said, "I can feel it in my bones, we will be grandparents within the year." Friends and family suggested that the title, "Grandfather" was too difficult for little ones to pronounce. This made Harvey all the more determined ruffling his feathers even more. My sister Sheilla declared, "They will never call you grandfather, they will call you whatever comes to their little minds." "You just wait and see," Harvey replied with an unwavering voice.

No one was aware of Harvey's previous power of prayer for children. Laura told us that they had no immediate plans to start a family. She and Tim had established positions working in Northern Virginia, plus they had just purchased their first home.

Unbeknownst to Laura and Tim, Harvey had already offered up prayers for a grandchild. A few months passed and we received a phone call from Laura. She started with just some small talk about getting settled and how much they loved their new home. Suddenly, her voice changed to a higher pitch, "Mom, Dad, you're going to have a grandchild!" Laura admitted that they were just as surprised as we were, but Harvey was not really surprised at all. He had asked God already and expected this blessing. Within a couple of hours most of our family and friends heard about our exciting news. Knowing the power of prayer, Harvey had consistently prayed for a grandchild.

Wyatt Read Hamilton made his way into the world kicking and screaming with arms open. Harvey had prayed fervently and even had put in a request for a grandson. Of course, he would accept a granddaughter, but he knew the power of prayer. Tim helped Laura stay comfortable while in labor and then helped with the delivery and volunteered to cut the cord. He was much braver than Harvey who did not watch, did not help, and just enjoyed the results!! Wyatt was the most beautiful baby boy we had ever seen. Laura and Tim were beaming and so happy that God had given them this precious child. Harvey and I and Lyle and Mary Ann, Laura's parents were so happy to be able to share in the birth of our first grandson together.

When Harvey told Laura that he wanted the grandchildren to call him "Grandfather" she suggested that it may be difficult for them to pronounce and that they may call him something else instead. Harvey would talk to Wyatt as if he were talking to an adult, no baby talk for him. Wyatt developed his own little language which sounded like gibberish to everyone except his grandfather. Grandfather Harvey would listen and answer Wyatt back. Sometimes, Harvey would point to himself and say, "Grandfather;" he was determined that Wyatt would call his name. Although Wyatt's first word was "Daddy," one day he suddenly blurted out "Grandfather!" His enunciation was perfect. Harvey proudly smirked, and said, "I told you so; I knew he would say the big 'G' word."

29: *The Grandfather*

Wyatt and his grandfather became extremely attached to one another. One day when Wyatt was about a year and a half old, he made me laugh myself silly. He loved eating goldfish crackers from the bag. I told him, "You only get one." His serious little eyes looked up at me and he said, "Can I have two ones?" He was so smart and so clever. His sweet disposition constantly put a smile on my face.

There were times when Grandfather Harvey would put Wyatt on his lap while at the piano and play a little tune. He would take Wyatt's little finger and pluck the keys, forcing loud giggles from him. There were times when Wyatt would lay on the floor on his stomach, with his chin cupped cutely in his hands as he intently watched his grandfather play the guitar as if he understood every note. Those two monkeys delighted in each other and their relationship grew and became even more special.

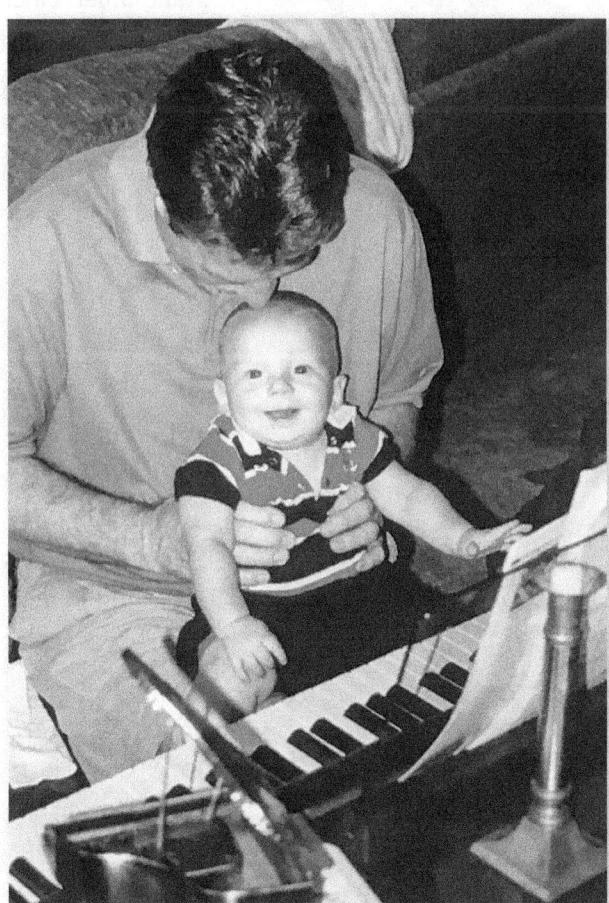

"Grandfather is so much fun"

WHY GOD WHY?

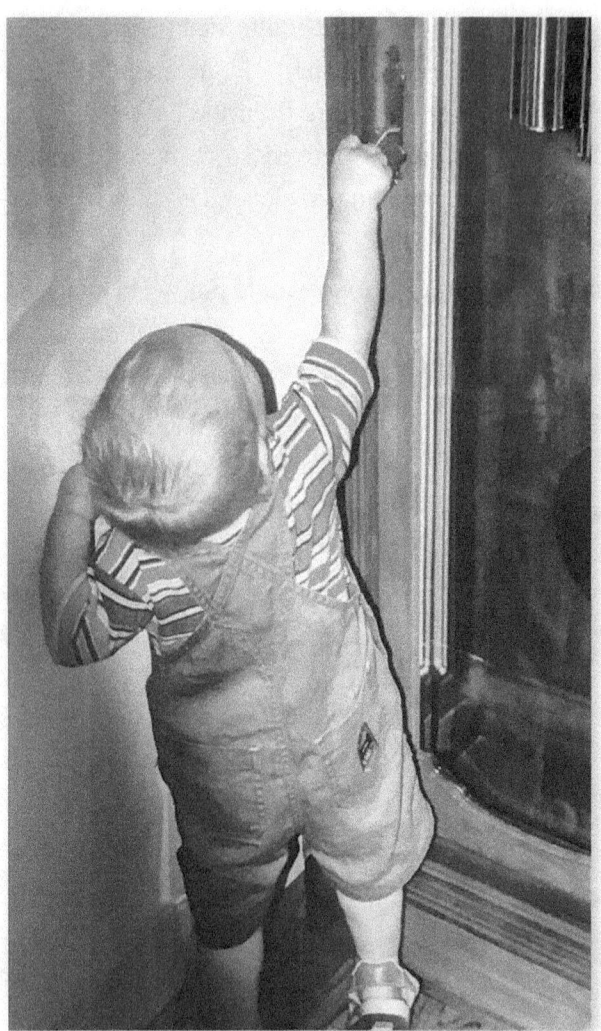

"Now, let me get this right," says Wyatt

Harvey started a tradition with Wyatt and it spilled over to the rest of the grandchildren later on. Years back, I had given Harvey a grandfather clock for his birthday, of which he was very protective. When Wyatt was about fifteen months old Harvey taught him how to retrieve the keys for the clock from the foyer drawer and very carefully open the door with the one key and wind the clock with the other key. Whenever the clock needed winding, Harvey would say to Wyatt, "Hurry, Grandson, the clock is running down and the weight is about to hit the floor." Wyatt would run, get the keys from the drawer, and stretch up high on his stool to reach the keyhole. Wyatt knew that he was never to touch the mechanisms inside of the clock, and he knew that the keys always had to be put back into the foyer drawer.

29: *The Grandfather*

Harvey didn't have to pray for the second grandchild. Laura and Tim decided to give Wyatt a little brother or sister to grow up with. Samuel Edward Hamilton, came into this world not so little. We were all shocked when Little Sammy arrived at almost 10 pounds, considerably outweighing Wyatt who weighed 6.7 pounds at birth. Laura and the doctor were so surprised they even weighed him a second time to make sure!!

Sammy was a big, armful of love. Harvey thought no one would be as wonderful as Wyatt, but he soon found out that Sammy was just as wonderful. Sammy had his own unique characteristics and good looks to boot. Wyatt took to Sammy right away, but it didn't take long before he wanted to drag him around like he did his stuffed animals.

Wyatt dragging Sammy like a stuffed animal

WHY GOD WHY?

Wyatt & Sammy make up and forgive inside the Hamilton Hideout

Things changed somewhat, in Sammy's toddler years. Wyatt knocked Sammy around as if he were a toy. To Wyatt's surprise, Sammy put himself into the body of a super hero and knocked Wyatt silly. Afterwards they made up and retreated into their cardboard clubhouse that mom had helped with. She gave it a name and wrote over the door, "The Hamilton Hideout."

Sammy was also attached to his grandfather like a bee to honey. This sometimes presented a problem when the boys would argue about who would sit next to grandfather. However, Sammy liked having his own space and was intrigued with putting things together. He was our little artistic thinker of the family. Wyatt, on the other hand, was uncommonly bright and productive, but he preferred having someone around to share with.

Both boys' love for their grandfather continued to grow and has always been very special. Of course, they love me, too. However, my role as grandmother is the disciplinarian, and I serve with a servant's heart. Of course, being the grandmother does have its advantages; the grandchildren loved my cooking and the stories I would tell, as they cuddled up by

29: The Grandfather

me on the sofa before bedtime. At naptime or bedtime, the grands always loved my story telling—created in my mind as I told it. Harvey loves to entertain the children all day doing whatever they want to do, not what he wants to do. He gives of himself unselfishly. He is the grownup playmate who never tires. He even lets them stay up late just to have more time with them. There are times I disagree with that, but then oftentimes I am reminded of Mary and Martha, who were friends of Jesus. While Harvey was playing with the boys, I was cooking and cleaning and busy doing work around the house. The best part was after I was done everything, it was my turn to play. There is nothing more wonderful than playing with your grandchildren and hearing their laughter.

We not only became Grandfather and Grandmother to our grandchildren, but we were always delighted when we would receive Christmas cards from some of the families in the neighborhood addressed to Grandfather and Grandmother—and they were actually delivered to us in the mail.

One afternoon, Harvey and I were having coffee on our deck sharing our thoughts when he announced—"Honey, we need a little grand-girl!" My mouth dropped open as I sternly told him that he should not mention that to Laura and Tim. He never did, however, he commissioned Wyatt and Sammy to ask their mom for a little sister. Laura let Grandfather know that they had all they children they needed, but Harvey didn't let up. He kept sending the boys with the same message and kept praying for a granddaughter. Remembering what happened when he prayed for our son, and then when he prayed for our first grandson, it left me a little anticipative. Now he was preparing and planning for a little girl as if it was a definite thing.

A couple of months later, Laura called and wanted us to meet her for lunch. We often met at Panera Bread, so there was no reason to think there was anything special about this time. When she got there she announced with a grin, "Tim and I decided we are going to try for another little one."

That announcement was no surprise to Harvey. He excitedly said, "Yes, a grand-girl!" Laura gently and sweetly said, "The gender will be whatever God decides to give us."

Just like magic for the third time, Eleanor Ann Hamilton, who we call Nora, graced us with her presence four years after Sammy was born. Of course, to us she was the sweetest little girl package that God had ever put together! We felt so blessed to have another little one to love, and she was such an answer to Harvey's prayer. He smiled and said, "Ask and you shall receive. If you want a girl, ask specifically."

The boys loved playing with Nora. They would all cuddle on the floor and put toys around her while trying to get her to talk. They especially loved to read stories to her and she looked as if she really understood every word. Although Nora was her daddy's little princess, she was mommy's little playmate. Nora absolutely loved her Grandfather. They had a special love and bond that was extraordinary. In fact, she demanded so much attention that the boys had to share a lot of the time. She loved her Grandmother, too. Whenever she was hurt or got very serious about something she would come to me. As Nora grew older, keeping up with the boys seemed very easy for her, until the day she tried to empty her bladder in the woods, just like the boys ... oops!

When the grandchildren were younger, Harvey decided to build them a treehouse. He even added a front porch. He loved visiting them in the treehouse and all the children helped with their ideas. Granddaddy Lyle also had a hobby with woodworking projects and built the grands many wonderful things that they will never forget. He was an avid hunter and fisherman, and he taught the boys to love camping, especially cooking their catch over the fire. Tim taught the boys to hunt skillfully and safely. Tim and Laura also loved to be outdoors and raised their family to be very outdoorsy. They would go hiking, horseback riding, play tennis and they loved

29: *The Grandfather*

Wyatt, Nora & Sam mother 'Si,' their duck

to ski. Other things they enjoyed doing were going zip-lining and hunting. The family, one and all, loved and shared in water and snow skiing.

Harvey likes to take every opportunity he can to spend time with the grandkids. Whenever Laura needs him to pick up the kids from school, even when he is tired, he immediately gets a burst of energy and is excited he will be seeing the grand kids. Grandfather loves it when we lunch with the grands at school. We especially love to attend their sporting events and practices whenever we can. Laura's mother, Mary Ann (Weezy) Lacy, is the other grandmother who loves spending time with the grands. Their granddaddy, Lyle, passed on with cancer, but not before teaching the grands many things about hunting, fishing, camping and how to live life to the fullest.

Harvey and I have certainly been blessed with such a wonderful family. Tim and Laura have given us the most special gift in the world.

WHY GOD WHY?

There is nothing more wonderful than having grandchildren; we are so fortunate that we can share time with them often. Our grandchildren have been taught to give praise and be thankful to the Lord for all their blessings. My grandmother pride is overwhelming as I hear each one of them praying their prayers at bedtime when they say, "Dear Lord, thank you for Mom, Dad, Grandad, Weezy, Grandmother, Grandfather, Uncle Matt and Aunt Kristen and especially for Jesus." There is no sound more wonderful than hearing our grandchildren say our names—Nora sometimes calls me "Gram" and she calls Harvey "Gramph"—but his favorite name of all is still Grandfather.

Chapter 30
WHEN YOU THINK YOU HAVE TROUBLES

There are people across this world devastated from lack of shelter, food, family, security, and most of all, the Lord. Twelve years ago, Harvey and I started a foundation intended to aid tragedy-stricken and deprived people.

On his first trip to Nicaragua, Harvey witnessed the ghastly results of a disaster that impacted him deeply; so horribly that he could not discuss it over the phone. Deep emotions filled the receiver each time he started to describe the scenes.

After returning and settling back home, Harvey shared unimaginable sites that he observed first hand. A week or two before his trip to Nicaragua, monsoon rains created rivers and mudslides, which poured down the mountains. The natives below had reason to worry about their villages flooding. Without any let-up, the rains continued until the mountaintop volcano filled with hot boiling water. No one was aware that the lava was hot enough to boil rainwater to unspeakable degrees. Without forewarning, the volcano erupted, forcing rivers of lava, boiling water and mud down the mountain burning and killing everything in its path. This unexpected catastrophe wiped out entire villages and completely charred families, animals, gardens, fruit trees and more.

WHY GOD
WHY?

Harvey went with a small group to an area that had become a gigantic gravesite, covering miles of land. By this time, authorities had already removed many recognizable human bodies. The waters were still rapidly running into rivers carrying carcass parts of many kinds, items, and debris from villages. Harvey photographed a family of a father, mother and their child clinging together. Their bodies were charred to the bone and hardly recognizable. The picture Harvey painted of this tragedy has stayed with me, to reflect on when I think times are tough.

Harvey met a pastor whose family and church is supported by one of our clients, a wonderful lady with a mission. Although the pastor's family did not have much to offer, they humbly invited Harvey and his friend to dinner and shared the little they had. Harvey learned to love their frijoles and rice. He said they reminded him of the old lady in the Bible, who only had two pence, and gave it all. The children in the family worked very hard to help maintain the little farm. Although this family was in great sorrow, for the loss of the people, their love and care for all humankind was evident.

Harvey was so caught up in the needs and suffering of the people in Nicaragua that he insisted I join him on the next trip that would be a few weeks later. Our friend, Beverly, who supports the church joined us there, on the return trip. Her agenda was to buy the church a new automobile to continue delivering food to the poor helpless ones in the mountains; their old auto died.

The taxi driver drove us down a shabby part of town where we saw a U.S.A. school bus overloaded with people. They were hanging out of the doors and windows, as if their lives depended on getting to a destination. When I asked, "Why are we in such a bad part of town," I was shocked with the answer, "This is the good part of town."

Previously, Nicaragua was deprived by a mutinous dictator, and his subordinates, who robbed the country of their resources. They had no

30: When You Think You Have Troubles

capital to assist or care for all the people. Therefore, they robbed the people of what little they had. When we visited a very needy children's hospital, it was evident how poor they were. They had no proper medical equipment, or sheets to put between the children and cold, rubber mattresses. The children were very sick and needed, at the very least, some comfort. These conditions saddened us enormously. We stood over a baby who was sick. The lack of medical equipment led the caretakers to supply oxygen by placing a large, clear, plastic bowl over the child's face, and inserting a small rubber hose under the bowl to pipe in air. Most of the children there had no families to retrieve them. The older children sat along the walls moaning and sobbing. Beverly insisted on buying these sick children sheets for their beds. We all pitched in and dressed the beds throughout the hospital.

That first evening, we drove into the mountains to visit our pastor and his family, then attended their church nearby. Some of these people were still hurting from the loss of friends who died in the volcanic eruption. Most were poor and lived in small, one-room structures or huts. However, when we walked into the church and saw the excitement on their faces, we truly witnessed the presence of the Holy Spirit. The stage band was playing praise songs that shouted out the name of Christ ("Christo"). People were dancing and lifting their hands toward heaven in an expression of faith and worship. Two of the pastor's sons were talented with music and had a couple of friends with the same instrument talent. Harvey saw their guitars and wanted to join them. It was not long until the pastor, asked him to come on stage and play music with them. As the village people praised God and sung for joy, it became contagious. I had never before been so excited and filled with the spirit of our Lord Jesus. These people were so poor in things, but rich in God's love which showed on their faces

Many of our Nicaraguan friends thought it was exciting that we lived in a prosperous free country like America. While traveling to the airport,

Harvey and I shared our feelings about the blessings of living in the greatest nation on earth. Yes, at times we take our blessings and opportunities for granted. "Honey," I said, "let us always thank our Lord for His grace and mercy, to a nation founded by a praying people, to a living God; 'One Nation under God.'"

I was not afraid of flying on the return trip. After the experiences of the past couple of days, I could certainly take flying in a huge, comfortable aircraft with food and beverages. When I begin to complain of my problems, I think of those who are hungry, cold and have no family or place to call home. As I gazed at all the stars, I prayed, "Lord, teach us to love and care for others as You love and care for us; and may we be thankful for our many blessings each day."

Chapter 31
DO IT AGAIN, GRANDFATHER!

Harvey had reminded me on several occasions, "If you don't fly with us, you are going to miss out on many trips with your grandchildren." Certainly, I will not miss out on the ones I can drive to. And, that is just what I did on this trip.

Our daughter-in-law, Laura, and the grandsons flew off with Grandfather to Myrtle Beach. Tim had to stay home and take care of business. I was well on my way, cruising down the highway alone. They would arrive there in an hour, while my driving would take five and a half hours. Harvey doesn't miss an opportunity to throw that in my face. He detests riding hours cramped up in a car.

By the time I arrived, they were all settled in the condo, snacking, laughing and getting ready for the pool. It wasn't the warmest day, but that did not deter those children. We had a few great days with the little munchkins and Laura. They certainly brought joy to this Myrtle Beach trip. When you're having fun at the beach, time moves by so fast. I drove to the airport and waved them off before I hit the road again—alone again.

It was a very windy day and became even more robust the closer I got to home. Listening to radio reports about damaging winds triggered me to pray for the children. With faith and confidence, I turned them over to the

WHY GOD WHY?

Lord. None of the children would have been as jumpy as Grandmother, had I been flying with them.

I was about two hours from home when the wind became horrific. With both hands, it was all I could do to hold the car on the road. Harvey has said that I am the only female driver that he feels safe with. He should have seen the intenseness going on as I sat up straight. The wind seemed to move the car off the road at times. Most drivers were creeping along like Granny Grunts. However, I wanted to get home and see the children. I should not have been traveling so fast.

Finally, I made it to Greensboro. I knew the children had been home hours before. However, I was still happy to be on the ground and not in the air. The first thing I heard when I turned the radio on was, "Aircraft, owned by a local, had a mishap on the runway at the Regional Airport in Lynchburg!" My brain decided not to assume it was Harvey and the family. I knew he should have already landed by now. "So, dear Lord, I am turning the family over to you for protection, either way. I'm keeping the faith, knowing that You have it all under control."

My bladder was full, and I needed to make a stop, but my foot seemed glued to the gas pedal. It was then that I received a call from my sister, asking me about Harvey's accident at the airport. "Did you say Harvey's accident?" I anxiously asked. "Oh no, you haven't heard?" was her response. It had been on the news.

About ten minutes later, I was happy to receive a call from Harvey. He wanted to inform me of the accident before I heard it from the media announcements. "Everyone is okay, and I want you to take your time and drive safely," he assured me. Harvey usually doesn't like to go into detail; however, he did relay most of the accident details. He said the wind was so forceful when they began to descend for the landing. Very skillfully, Harvey had to control his steering while the plane swung back and forth. Immediately upon touchdown, the front wheel collapsed and rolled back up under the airplane. With force, the nose of the plane collapsed and slid down the runway throwing sparks all the way. When they finally came to a complete stop, Little Sammy had just awakened and yelled, "Do it again Grandfather!"

"Come on, Grandfather"

Sammy's remark completely changed the tenseness in the cabin. Emergency crews and fire truck sirens were blaring as the firemen opened the door. When they saw everyone inside laughing, they knew they were okay. Each one in my family climbed out of the aircraft. They were safe and sound. The news media was already there ready to ask questions.

I was happy that Harvey had called and explained everything to me. I was thanking the Lord for answering my prayers and bringing the family home safely. The Bible says our mind is the battlefield, where the evil one tries to fill us with doubts and fears. He didn't get to me this time; I didn't tremble in fear, I talked with the Lord who was near.

WHY GOD WHY?

I couldn't wait to get home to give them all hugs and listen to the family excitement and their joy of being safe and sound.

Grandfather's love of flying became contagious. Laura was so interested in flying that she took flying lessons and attained her pilot's license not long after moving to the area. Tim had learned to fly when Harvey flew him back and forth to college. This became an adventure and a means of travel that the family and many friends have enjoyed. Our grandson, Wyatt, took an interest in flying; grandfather would have it no other way. They say there is safety in numbers. With many Hamilton flights, including a couple of scary ones, our team pools their resources, and takes to the air.

Laura flying
Tim & Wyatt

Chapter 32
DID YOU EVER WONDER WHY?

Looking out at all the beautiful birds on the porch railing reminds me of the Bible verse where it says, if God feeds and takes care of these small creatures, how much more does God care for us, whom He created in His own image?

For everyone, life is a journey planned by God. When we marry our God-given mate, we two become one, and our individual plans entwine. Together, our faith was strengthened as we became part of a triangle moving toward Jesus. Suffering on one's journey is inevitable; their response is a choice. Whether on a mountaintop high or valley low, our faith and attitude defines who we are in Christ.

Our family has survived an unusual number of grief-stricken valley lows on our journey. Unequivocally, Harvey and I would not have made it through, and still be together, without having a personal relationship with the Lord Jesus. Our mountaintop blessings have been many, however, we didn't appreciate them until we spent time in the valley. We learned that the valley experiences were temporary, and stood on Psalm 121:8, *"The Lord will guard your goings and coming from this time and forever."*

In my deepest times of pain and despair, I would call out to the Holy Spirit for guidance. Each time He reached down to pull me up, I felt His deep scars as though they were inflicted on me. There were times I wondered why we had to endure so many valley experiences. However, we have been blessed to know that others, with painful experiences, have come to know the Lord, by hearing our story. As we grew in Jesus, we learned to give God the glory and concentrate more on our blessings.

Tim, Laura and the grandchildren are blessings and have added so much to our lives. They taught us that life is not about waiting for the storm to pass, it's about learning to dance in the rain and be thankful all the while.

Our son sacrificed so much to take care of all the family. His love for us and his level of intelligence brought us through some tough times; although, it probably didn't do much for his health. It took a loving, beautiful person like Laura to help through such a transition. She is a lively package of smarts and spirit, with a can-do attitude. She's also a live wire who doesn't believe in the words, can't and quit. I think she is the person who invented the phrase, "When life gives you lemons, make lemonade."

Tim and Laura have taught the children to love others, be humble, take responsibility, and thank God each day for their blessings. You might see them planting a veggie garden with Laura or four-wheeling with Tim or the whole family in the hot tub singing to the stars. Family time is a big thing around the Hamilton household.

Tim and his family have filled our life with complete joy. I laugh when I think of how we strived to care for and educate our children. Now, they try to do the same for us. It's exciting as we learn from each other, and individually move into God's plan for our lives. We don't have to create a legacy to leave behind; our children and grandchildren are our treasured legacies, without question.

We are learning to submit more to the Lord. We don't have to wonder—Why? God knows where we are at all times, and why we are allowed to be there. Thank goodness for the Holy Spirit, our Comforter, and Guide. He has been there all along helping to point us in the right direction—we just have to allow Him. Some of us take so long to realize that His strength and guidance is always for our good. We can rejoice wherever we are in life. 'In The Valley, He Restoreth My Soul,' was a favorite song that helped me along the way.

James 1:3—*"Consider it all joy, my brethren, when you encounter various trials, knowing that the testing of your faith produces endurance. And let endurance have its perfect result so that you may be perfect and complete, lacking nothing."*

To God be the glory!

Our active blessings: Tim, Laura, Wyatt, Sammy and Nora

2013—Violet P. Hamilton

ABOUT THE AUTHOR

Violet Perry Hamilton was born in Lynchburg, Virginia during World War II, on September 30, 1943. She was the second of four children born to Paul, an electrician, and his dedicated wife, Arlene.

In 1963, a year after high school graduation, Violet married her longtime sweetheart, Harvey Hamilton. She joined him in Massachusetts, where he was stationed in the US Air Force, and they later transferred to Bossier City, Louisiana.

While in the Air Force, both Violet and Harvey were able to continue their education at Louisiana Tech. After Harvey was honorably discharged from the USAF, they moved back to Lynchburg, where Violet took a position in the Information Technology division of Jerry Falwell

Ministries, including the *Old Time Gospel Hour*, while Harvey worked for a well-established music company. They both furthered their education at Liberty University and the local community college simultaneously. Violet's work ethic and love for technology led the ministry to further her education in Atlanta, Georgia.

In 1986, after much prayer, Violet and Harvey founded a Marketing/Information Management service company, Valtim, which has grown and prospered and served well-known entities around the world. The Hamilton's have always given the Lord the glory for the business and have relied on His direction through its ups and downs.

Now semi-retired, the Hamilton's have passed the torch of leadership of Valtim to their son, Tim, and are enjoying their three wonderful grandchildren. Harvey continues with aspects of the business, while Violet has focused on her love of writing. This is her first published volume.

www.ingramcontent.com/pod-product-compliance
Lightning Source LLC
LaVergne TN
LVHW051832080426
835512LV00018B/2834